MW01492961

GARDENS OF TEXAS

GARDENS OF TEXAS

Visions of Resilience from the Lone Star State

PAM PENICK

Photography by Kenny Braun

TIMBER PRESS
Portland, Oregon

OPPOSITE: Texas gayfeather and pine muhly burst into flower in Plano.

Timber Press
Workman Publishing
Hachette Book Group, Inc.
1290 Avenue of the Americas
New York, New York 10104
timberpress.com

Timber Press is an imprint of Workman Publishing, a division of Hachette Book Group, Inc. The Timber Press name and logo are registered trademarks of Hachette Book Group, Inc.

Printed in Dongguan, China (TLF), on responsibly sourced paper

Text design by Sarah Crumb and Sara Isasi; Illustrations by Sara Isasi
Cover design by Sarah Crumb

The publisher is not responsible for websites (or their content) that are not owned by the publisher.

The Hachette Speakers Bureau provides a wide range of authors for speaking events. To find out more, go to hachettespeakersbureau.com or email hachettespeakers@hbgusa.com.

ISBN 978-1-64326-374-8

A catalog record for this book is available from the Library of Congress.

To Aaron and Julia,
my born-and-raised Texans,
with hope, always,
for a life well lived in this beautiful world of ours.

And to David for everything.

CONTENTS

PREFACE

GARDENING IN TEXAS, as anyone knows who's tried it, is wholly different from gardening in other parts of the United States. Our seasons tend to be upside-down in terms of when to plant, when to prune, when to harvest … and when to go inside to read a book or binge a show until gardening weather returns. It's no wonder new gardeners and newcomers to Texas often struggle to find their footing.

Elsewhere, May might be prime time for planting, but in Texas, temps can soar to triple digits by then, shriveling transplants fresh out of their nursery pots. We don't put our gardens to bed for winter either. (What does that even mean?) Throughout much of the state, gardens remain quite green all winter thanks to an evergreen canopy of live oak, juniper, palmetto, Texas mountain laurel, and magnolia; shrubs like holly, Texas sage, and agarita; and dry-loving plants like yucca, sotol, agave, hesperaloe, and prickly pear. In warmer parts of the state, gardeners can harvest cool-season vegetables and citrus all winter, if they protect plants from the occasional freeze.

Texas gardeners hit the ground running in February and March, feverishly pruning and planting and watching spring swiftly unfold. Flowering trees (redbuds, plums, Texas mountain laurel) start the show, followed by our beloved native wildflowers (Texas bluebonnet, Indian paintbrush, columbine, pink evening primrose). Shrubs and subshrubs (from spirea to autumn sage) and perennials (rock rose, salvia, Turk's cap, lantana) soon erupt in a flash mob of color. By June the heat is fully on, but our gardens, especially if nourished by spring rains, continue their rampant growth under the blazing sun. In the West Texas desert, long-awaited monsoon rains arrive in June, shifting the gardening seasons even more.

By midsummer, Texas gardeners may retreat indoors or park themselves under a porch fan with a cold drink to wait for fall. Summer chores like watering, weeding, and mowing get relegated to early morning or evening. The long, broiling summer tests the endurance of plants and gardeners alike.

At last, the first autumn rain and flag-snapping north breeze drops temperatures below 90 degrees—a seasonal shift as sweetly anticipated as the spring thaw in colder climates. Though gardens may be a little crispy or wilted at summer's end (or pre-monsoon in West Texas), they quickly perk up and burst into flower again. Fall, our bountiful second spring, has arrived.

Whale's tongue agave, blackfoot daisy, 'Blonde Ambition' blue grama, and Gregg dalea sparkle against a dark-limbed live oak in Linda Peterson's San Antonio garden.

Vastness defines our state. Texas ranks as the largest state in the contiguous United States, spanning 268,000 square miles and USDA Hardiness Zones 6b to 10b. To drive across it, you'll put about 800 miles under your wheels. While all of Texas is part of the southern Great Plains, its diversity is signified by ten ecoregions officially designated by the Texas Parks and Wildlife Department: the sandy soil Pineywoods; slow-draining Gulf Prairies and Marshes; scattered oak grassland of the Post Oak Savanna; fertile Blackland Prairie; tree-belted Crosstimbers; thornscrub of the South Texas Plains; spring-dripping canyons of the Edwards Plateau; shortgrass prairie of the Rolling Plains; windy plateau of the High Plains; and the Trans-Pecos, encompassing desert valleys, wooded slopes, and rocky peaks of the Guadalupe and Davis Mountains. Elevations range from sea level along the Gulf Coast to 8751 feet atop Guadalupe Peak. Rainfall varies wildly too, from a yearly average of 60 inches in the southeastern part of the state to a scant 10 inches in the westernmost city of El Paso. With so much variation of topography and climate, there is no one-size-fits-all gardening advice for Texans.

Challenges abound for the Texas gardener: extreme heat, drought, floods, hurricanes, the occasional multiday freeze, thorny plants in abundance, rattlesnakes, and, not least, fire ants. Still, Texans are up for a challenge, and we like to grow things. We garden for fresh food, to beautify our homes, to create habitat for wildlife, to conserve native plants, to create sanctuaries for ourselves, to cool our yards and cities, to express ourselves creatively, to be outdoors with hands in the dirt, and for any other reason you can think of. Responding to the state's natural cycles of drought and flood, Texans were early adopters of sustainable practices like growing native plants, converting thirsty lawns into waterwise gardens, and collecting rainwater and managing runoff. We treasure our native plants, especially our wildflowers, among which the bluebonnet reigns supreme as our official state flower. The official state botanic garden, the Lady Bird Johnson Wildflower Center in Austin, is devoted entirely to Texas native plants.

With a rich palette of native and well-adapted nonnative plants to choose from, we make beautiful, interesting, and distinctively Texan gardens. I've had the pleasure of visiting scores of Texas gardens over the years on tours and via invitations from fellow gardeners, designers, and those on social media, many of whom I've connected with through my blog, *Digging* (penick.net). I learn a little more about gardening in Texas from each garden I visit.

Despite our state's vibrant gardening culture, I've found that many garden books, magazines, and online sources written for a national audience feature mostly gardens along the East Coast and West Coast—not the Third Coast, as Texas is sometimes called. Those deservedly admired gardening regions do boast a wealth of stunning gardens. But I'm often frustrated that Texas gardens are not

Open desert grassland and the Davis Mountains make an epic borrowed view in Jim Martinez and Jim Fissel's garden in Marfa.

better represented. That absence is one of the reasons I started my blog back in 2006—to share the reality of gardening in Texas and to foster conversations about gardening in this unique region. And that's why I've written this book. After many years of wishing for a book featuring a multitude of Texas gardens, showcasing the beauty, creative design, sustainability practices, and gardening passion across our vast state, I realized that I just needed to write it myself.

A rainbow arcs over Susan Kirr and
Rusty Martin's Marfa garden after
a monsoon rain shower.

As I started working on this book in January 2023, one question concerned me: would anyone be willing to share their garden for publication so soon after our state had been battered by a series of severe weather events? Across Texas, gardeners were smarting from one pummeling after another. Two winters prior, in February 2021, Winter Storm Uri walloped Texas with a week of subfreezing temperatures and snow, plus a multiday loss of power and water affecting millions. Apart from the significant human toll, landscaping across the state took a hit, as certain trees, shrubs, and dryland plants like agaves—the most valuable and defining plants in many gardens—were lost to the zone-smashing cold. In 2022, another deep freeze occurred, finishing off many plants still in recovery after Uri. Next, a broiling summer tested our gardens. In early 2023, a devastating ice storm struck Central Texas, where I live, snapping mature trees and knocking out power lines for a week. And then came the heat-wave summer of 2023, the second-hottest summer on record for Texas, and *the* hottest on record for many Texas cities. By the time you read this, those records may have fallen to new ones.

None of this has been easy on our gardens. Under such circumstances, it might have made sense to hold off a year or two on photographing gardens for this book, in hopes that the next year would be milder, the rains would come when needed, and the owners of every garden featured here would know that their garden had never looked better. Unfortunately, we can't count on normal weather patterns anymore, if we ever could. Our climate is changing. Weather is more unpredictable than it used to be. High temperatures are hotter and last longer. Deep freezes, though typically brief, are surprising us more often. Droughts are deepening, even as rainstorms and hurricanes are growing more intense, bringing a higher likelihood of flooding. Even for experienced gardeners, hard-won knowledge about gardening in Texas is being thrown into question. We're all wondering, which plants can we rely on to survive longer, hotter summers but also an occasional stretch of single-digit freezes? That can thrive in a scorching, rainless summer but also slog through when a storm dumps inches of rain in a few hours? How should we be preparing our gardens for future extremes so that we can still have a beautiful place that brings us joy and satisfaction and has a positive impact on our environment?

These questions were on my mind as I talked with each garden owner and designer featured in these pages. I believe we draw strength and inspiration from seeing what other gardeners are accomplishing and how they're adapting to these changes—because we're *all* adapting our gardens as they're tested anew each year. We're figuring things out together. And although many of the gardens featured here were recently thinned by Mother Nature's hand, their owners are still looking forward, still finding joy in gardening, and remain generous about sharing them.

Texans are a diverse lot, and so are the gardens we're growing across this marvelously varied state. Within these pages are featured an assortment of beautiful Texas gardens and their creators, as well as their stories of how the gardens came to be, the value they draw from them, and how they're adapting to changing conditions. For some, the garden represents the sublime beauty of nature, curated at their doorstep. For others, it's an artistic pursuit to make pleasing compositions of plants and ornament. For still others, it's a way of carrying on treasured memories, or benefitting wildlife and endangered plants, or putting healthy food on the table. Or all of these things at once. As every gardener who has been at it a while knows, there is no final moment of perfection in a garden, no end goal. It's not about that. Gardening is about the doing and the growing, resowing and replanting, and looking to the future, while enjoying the innumerable, ephemeral moments of delight a garden offers in the present.

That's what I hope to convey with this compilation of gardens from Nacogdoches to Fort Davis and from Grapevine to Edinburg. I am honored to have been welcomed into each one of these deeply personal gardens, each one transcendent in its own way, each one carrying on despite the challenges of the toughest summers and winters on record. I hope these essays and photographs will enchant, inspire, and encourage you in your own gardening pursuits. Yes, our familiar climate is changing. Yes, gardening in Texas is more challenging than ever. And yes, we can still make meaningful, wildlife-friendly, productive, and gorgeous gardens.

Just turn the pages and see. You'll find 27 private gardens, including one family farm, from cities and towns across Texas. The book is divided into five sections corresponding to five broad geographical regions of the state: Central Texas, West Texas, South Texas, North Texas, and East Texas. Each section features between five and seven gardens located within that region. For each garden, you'll find an essay drawn from interviews with the owner or designer, multiple pages of photos, and an idea page with a design or gardening tip and recommended plants from the garden.

I hope you enjoy this garden tour across Texas.

Wildflowers echo the Austin skyline
in Ruthie Burrus's hilltop garden.

CENTRAL
TEXAS

THE PLACE

Central Texas is a place of rock and natural springs. Wooded canyons stubbled with exposed limestone. Dripping caverns festooned with maidenhair ferns. Green, spring-fed creeks and rivers, where knobby-kneed bald cypresses wade in the shallows. The Blackland Prairie rolling up to the cliffs of the Balcones Escarpment, an ancient fault line where the rugged Hill Country begins.

CLIMATE

Semiarid to humid subtropical. Summers are long, hot, and humid, and winters are mild, although hard freezes can be expected. Rainfall occurs throughout the year and averages between 30 and 35 inches annually, although drought is common.

CHALLENGES AHEAD

Summers are growing hotter and lasting longer, and droughts are expected to intensify. Rainfall may remain at similar levels but fall with greater intensity, causing runoff and flash flooding. Winters are growing warmer overall but may bring more extreme cold snaps.

TAKE ACTION

☐ Install gutters and cisterns to collect and store rainwater.

☐ Install drip irrigation, which is less wasteful and more targeted than overhead sprinklers. Drip is sometimes exempt from municipal watering restrictions because of its efficiency.

☐ Choose native plants, which evolved to survive the weather extremes of their native range, and well-adapted nonnatives that can tolerate record highs and lows, not just average temps.

☐ Add rain gardens to manage runoff. Install terracing or check dams on slopes to hold rainwater and give it time to soak into the soil.

☐ Create shade by planting trees on the southwest and southeast sides of the garden and by building pergolas or installing shade sails over patios.

☐ Plant a prairie garden instead of lawn, where appropriate.

☐ Practice fire-wise landscaping if you live near woods, grassland, or canyon.

HANDS-IN-THE-DIRT GARDEN

"THE NUMBER-ONE RULE in my garden is, if you don't want to live here, you cannot live here," declares Ruthie Burrus. "So if a plant is not happy, I don't fight it because there are so many plants that *do* want to be here." Her garden is proof of that. Situated on a hilltop overlooking downtown Austin's skyscrapers on one side and glinting Lake Austin on another, it displays a confetti-bright mix of wildflowers, spiny agave and yucca, and romantic swaths of perennials and roses flowering pink and purple. "My garden is abundant with flowers," says Ruthie. "I don't plant too much that doesn't flower, so I have a lot of perennials. And you can imagine how many pounds of wildflower seeds I have distributed over eleven years."

The garden is most colorful in spring and fall, when milder temperatures and rain nudge plants into prolific bloom. "I love opening the garden to people during those times," says Ruthie. "It's gratifying, and it can be a teaching tool to educate people on native plants and organic gardening." Because she and husband Gene like to travel in summer, she doesn't plan specifically for hot-season flowers, and in winter the garden largely goes dormant. "This garden is very cyclical," explains Ruthie. "It can look like there's nothing planted in January and February because so many of my plants have gone underground. Sometimes people want to come see it then, and I say, 'Nope. Nope. Because you won't understand it if you don't see it in bloom.'"

Ruthie designed the 1-acre garden herself and fenced it to keep out the ever-present deer. (Another acre of the property, unfenced, was left natural for wildlife.) All along her steep, curving driveway, colorful swaths of native and exotic wildflowers—bluebonnets and pink evening primrose mingle with corn poppies and larkspur each spring—give an impression of nature just doing its thing. But that's by design. "Somebody was here and said, 'It's so nice how you left your whole hill wild,'" Ruthie says with a laugh. "And I was like, 'That hill is anything but wild. I spend more time on that hill than any part of my yard.'"

At the front of the house, Ruthie grows masses of foliage plants that tolerate dappled shade. Muscular, matte silver agaves thrust spiny arms toward glossy, lily pad–leaved giant leopard plant—an appealing, opposites-attract combo. Purple-flowering spiderwort draws in foraging bees. In back, where others might have gone minimalist and let the breathtaking views take center stage, Ruthie opted for maximalist and romantic. Using rust-colored rocks unearthed on the property, she and Gene cobbled together a charming stone shed, which Ruthie calls her garden *haus*—a nod to the German influence in the architecture of her Hill Country–style limestone home. Antique doors and windows and rusty corrugated roofing make the shed look like it has been standing for a hundred years. Pink roses hug the wall, and pink evening primrose sprawls below. From there, an undulating border of roses and salvia runs alongside a narrow lawn, adding color and pollinator habitat. In the center of the yard, a swimming pool and two covered porches—one for dining, the other for relaxing—provide relief from the summer sun. Just beyond, a long-eared bronze rabbit gazes out from a wilder

OPPOSITE: Ruthie's hilltop garden frames a view of downtown Austin.

FOLLOWING PAGE: A boisterous mix of native and adapted wildflowers brightens the winding driveway.

garden of native perennials, spiky-headed beaked yucca, and sword-like giant hesperaloe.

Ruthie gardened for 30 years in East Texas before moving to Austin. "Beaumont is a fabulous place to garden," she reminisces. "It's like gardening in a greenhouse. It's humid with tons of rain, and it's so easy to garden there." After relocating in 2009, she and Gene searched until they found the scenic hill with a flat top that was perfect for building their home. As she started making her new garden, Ruthie was surprised to discover how different conditions are compared to East Texas. "When I came here, I realized there wasn't going to be any rain. But I didn't realize there wasn't any dirt either," she says. "We're on 20 feet of rock, so we had to bring in 18 inches of dirt just to be able to plant stuff up here. It was totally opposite of Beaumont, with no dirt and no rain. I had to figure out plants that didn't need much of that."

Determined to collect whatever rainfall Mother Nature bestows, Ruthie and Gene installed a 10,000-gallon cistern just below the hilltop and a smaller cistern alongside the garden haus. Fed by runoff from the roof—channeled via gutters, rain chains, and underground pipes—the cisterns fill whenever it rains. The garden's irrigation system pulls from the harvested rainwater first, and when that runs low it switches to city water. "We did not drill a well because we thought it wasn't really in the spirit of things," says Ruthie. "We're trying to live within the constraints of this environment."

For Ruthie that means not just conserving water but choosing plants for pollinators and other wildlife. And while she's not a native plant purist—"there are too many cool plants out there," she says—native species make up a large percentage of her garden. She also sees her garden as an opportunity to show visitors—by opening to public tours and garden clubs—the rewards of gardening without resorting to toxic chemicals. "I think we have a job to do," Ruthie says emphatically. "We have a *job* to do. People don't realize that when they put weed-and-feed in their yard, it all runs down into the storm drains. They just don't know. A big part of it is just educating people." She also preaches about the importance of adding compost—not fertilizers—to create good soil. "I help a handful of people with their gardens, just as a friend," she says. "And invariably I can't get them to spend money on compost. They just want to stick the plants in the ground. One person had soil like concrete. You could barely get a shovel into it, it was that compacted. I kept saying, 'If you don't fix this soil …' He had these beautiful salvias, and they lasted two months. It's like your body: if it's not healthy on the inside, it won't look like it on the outside."

After thirteen years, Ruthie has noticed that extreme cold events in recent winters have made some plants, even natives, less reliable. "Some of my natives like four-nerve daisy just disappeared," she says. "And look at the Texas mountain laurels. They took a big hit. That's a little discouraging." Still, Ruthie doesn't dwell on plants that she's lost. And she vows not to replace any plant lost to a freeze more than once, even favorite evergreens like rosemary and 'Little Ollie' dwarf olive. "Plants that made it through are keepers," she says. "But plants I replaced after the big freeze of 2021 and then got hit again—those are *out*."

By focusing on the tough survivors, Ruthie makes peace with what's beyond her control. And she finds plenty to delight her in the plants that do thrive. "I love wandering around the garden," she says. "I love the sheer beauty. I love the connection with the earth. I think we need that. It's good to feel dirt in your hands." As a grandmother of eight, Ruthie takes every opportunity to pass on her love for the earth, often pointing out favorite wildflowers and teaching the kids their names. In her view, the stakes couldn't be higher. "We've screwed up this earth pretty well," she says, "and there's got to be a reversal. It's going to be up to the young people. They're the ones who are going to be the stewards."

ABOVE: A flagstone path lined with lamb's ear curves through a gravel garden of white-flowering and silvery plants.

LEFT: Ruthie Burrus constructed her romantic garden haus with antique doors and with stones unearthed from the property.

OPPOSITE: A bronze rabbit by sculptor Jim Budish stands among beaked yucca, Mexican bush sage, and heart-leaf skullcap.

ABOVE: A swimming pool edged with limestone reflects trees and sky.

RIGHT: On the covered back patio, a dining table offers an opportunity for a meal with a view.

ABOVE: The blue flowers of 'Mystic Spires' salvia appear in spring and last until frost.

LEFT: 'Climbing Pinkie' makes a romantic arch of pink roses on the garden haus.

OPPOSITE: 'Climbing Pinkie' rose clings to the rock wall of the garden haus. Silver- and white-flowering plants add a bit of Mediterranean style to a gravel garden.

LEFT: Native spiderwort and river fern thrive in the shade alongside a limestone vessel of water.

BELOW: A hummingbird swoops in to sample the spring banquet of wildflowers.

OPPOSITE, CLOCKWISE FROM TOP: A red-shouldered hawk soars over the garden.

Translucent petals and fuzzy stems of corn poppy glow in the wildflower meadow.

A honeybee makes for the violet flowers of native spiderwort.

Deepen the Foundation Bed

Often, a foundation bed hugs a super-skinny strip along the house, putting plants under the eave where rain doesn't fall and where they lack adequate room to grow. A more generous foundation bed gives plants space to mature without need of constant pruning to keep them in bounds. Plus, it looks in scale with the house and creates a more immersive experience as you walk through the garden to reach the door. Here are some tips.

» Make the planted area at least 6 to 8 feet deep. If space and resources permit, 10 to 12 feet is even better.

» Leave a 2- to 3-foot space unplanted along the house, which allows room for foundation inspections, window cleaning, painting, and other home upkeep. Lay mulch, gravel, flagstone, or pavers here to keep soil from splashing onto the siding when it rains.

» Choose plants whose mature size won't block your windows, except for taller accent shrubs or trees at the edges.

» Lay a wide and well-marked path to the front door so the house feels welcoming and accessible, not hidden behind a jungle of foliage.

» Consider adding a fountain or birdbath along the walk for the pleasant sight and sound of water.

Wildflower Meadow Plants for Central Texas

1/ **Texas bluebonnet** (*Lupinus texensis*): blue flowers in spring. This annual is easily grown from seed sown in gravelly soil.
2/ **Pink evening primrose** (*Oenothera speciosa*): sprawling, mounding perennial with masses of veined pink flowers. 3/ **Texas sotol** (*Dasylirion texanum*): strappy, sawtoothed, evergreen leaves keep the garden going after wildflowers fade. 4/ **Engel-mann's daisy** (*Engelmannia peristenia*): upright, cut-leaved stems with abundant yellow flowers. 5/ **Corn poppy** (*Papaver rhoeas*): nonnative but well-adapted annual with bright red flowers on hairy stems. 6/ **Winecup** (*Callirhoe digitata*): violet, cup-shaped, perennial flowers atop narrow, upright stems in spring. 7/ **Whale's tongue agave** (*Agave ovatifolia*): wide, cupped, blue-green leaves make this solitary agave beautiful all year, carrying the garden long after wildflowers have finished. 8/ **Mealy blue sage** (*Salvia farinacea*): tall stems topped with blue flower spikes, this perennial blooms spring through fall. 9/ **Larkspur** (*Consolida ambigua*): showy, nonnative annual wildflower with upright clusters of pink, white, lavender, or purple flowers.

TEXAS CREVICE GARDEN

WHEN THE COVID LOCKDOWN in 2020 shrank the world to his own home turf, Coleson Bruce found himself staring at a front lawn of neglected, parched St. Augustine grass. His midcentury ranch home in Austin was his first house, and it hadn't come with an instruction manual on yard care. "If there was anything smart to do about lawn, I didn't know it," says Coleson with a laugh. He only knew he didn't want anything that needed much water to thrive.

He'd been spitballing ideas with a gardening neighbor, John Ignacio, about redoing the yard to make it more water thrifty. John lobbed a suggestion: how about a crevice garden? Intrigued, Coleson delved online for more info. Crevice gardening, a new style of rock gardening that's growing in popularity, typically features alpine plants that prefer cool, dry summers. That wouldn't do for hot, muggy Central Texas. Still, Coleson was drawn to the sculptural form of a crevice garden, in which vertical slabs of stone are anchored in a gravelly berm like slices of toast in a rack. He started to envision a crevice garden that skewed southwestern, that took inspiration from the desert rather than alpine mountains. "I'm a desert rat," says Coleson. "I spent a lot of time in the Mojave Desert and in West Texas as a biology researcher before I became a lawyer."

Over the next six months, he collaborated with John on the garden, arranging truckloads of rocks and planting two crevice gardens, one in an existing island bed along the street and the other beside the front walk. Coleson worked obsessively, moving all but the biggest rocks himself and toiling long after dark by pointing his and his wife's trucks at the rockpile and flipping on the headlights. "Having a background in sculpture, the rockwork was the most innate part of gardening for me," he says. "Getting it to look natural, you have to think about how rocks run in the natural environment." Coleson relied on John's practiced eye for confirmation of his own intuition, which led once or twice to pulling everything up and starting over again. "I'd spend days moving tons of rocks," remembers Coleson. "In the back of my mind I'd think, 'That just doesn't look right.' John would show up the next day and look at it and say, 'That doesn't look right.' There were a couple instances where if I hadn't been prodded to take it apart and unwind days of work, it wouldn't be as good-looking as it is today."

As the crevice gardens came together, Coleson began eyeing the rest of the yard. He ripped out most of the lawn but kept a patch under a heritage live oak for a while longer, until that section got the shovel too. A loose layer of shredded wood mulch now protects the tree's root zone. He also yanked out an overgrown juniper hedge mustaching the front of the house. Suddenly, he and wife Elizabeth Geddes-Bruce needed screening for their exposed front windows. Coleson

OPPOSITE: Silver-green beaked yucca and silver ponyfoot harmonize in the gravel garden near the front door.

FOLLOWING PAGE: Low-growing perennials and small succulents sink their roots into the cool, deep crannies of the crevice garden.

decided to position clusters of beaked yucca in front of the house. Shrubby palms in the bermed crevice gardens added even more screening. To figure out plant placement, he and John made yucca and palm stand-ins using bamboo poles in 5-gallon buckets filled with sand. With poles of different lengths fanned out in a plant-like shape, they placed the buckets and walked up and down the street to see where privacy gaps opened up. "There was a period of time," says Coleson, "when the yard was stripped bare except for two or three dozen yellow buckets of bamboo poles. My neighbors must have thought I'd lost my mind." Today the palms are filling in slowly while the yuccas have grown so fast, soaring toward the roofline, that Coleson added a few smaller ones to retain privacy. The yuccas' strappy heads filter sunlight and shimmer in the breeze, making a pretty view from indoors while screening cars and houses. They require almost no irrigation and zero pruning.

As with any landscaping project, complications arose along the way. Of the six months it took him to build the garden, Coleson estimates at least half his time was spent repairing cracked PVC irrigation pipe and redesigning the whole system to fit his new garden's needs. "When you own an older house, god help you if you touch a shovel to the ground," says Coleson. "As soon as you plan to put something there, you'll find something else underground." Where he'd decided to plant some yuccas, a rusty, buried septic tank was found lurking like a hippo on a river bottom. Such snags bring out a layer of creativity, Coleson muses philosophically. "I think my yard would look very different today if I'd had an unfettered ability to put everything exactly where I thought it ought to go."

For Coleson, the garden's regular upkeep—tidying, shaping plants, editing the garden—puts him into a flow state where time is forgotten. "There are a handful of things in my life where, rather than glancing at the clock every five minutes and wondering how long it will be, I lift my head up and an entire day is gone," he says. Gardening is one of them. He also finds it's a way to spend time with his two boys, five-year-old Stanley James and three-year-old Cormac, who jump at every chance to help their dad. Seven-week-old daughter Matilda will, he hopes, join her brothers in the garden in a few years.

In 2021, the winter after the new garden was planted, Winter Storm Uri dumped more than 6 inches of snow, sealed that under an inch of ice, and locked Austin in a deep freeze for 144 hours straight, which included a record low of 6°F. A year later, another rare deep freeze struck. The following summer sizzled with 68 days of triple-digit temperatures and little rain. A few plants—barrel cacti, notably—turned to mush in the freezes. But overall Coleson has been pleased with the garden's survival rate. Crevice gardens lend themselves to protection from weather extremes, he says. "If it's cold out after a sunny day, rocks retain heat and create microclimates for plants to survive. In the summer, crevices are a cool, relatively moist place for plants' roots."

Now that the garden is more established, Coleson practices tough love. "I give new plants a little extra care for a year or two," he says. "But at some point, you've paid for college, and it's time for them to make it on their own." As for extreme weather brought on by the changing climate, Coleson takes a glass-half-full approach. "I see constraints as a sort of co-designer," he says. "It's a fun challenge to realize you've got to dig deeper into available plants and try new things, to see if a plant is among the rare jewels that can withstand a laser-beam sun for four months with very little water while also being able to handle a surprise four days of freezing temperatures. As extreme as our weather has been, there are lovely plants that lived up to expectations and are flourishing."

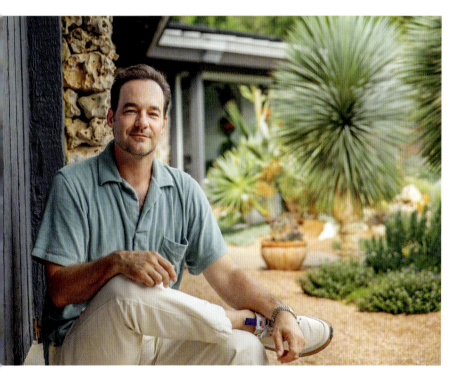

ABOVE: A drone view of the entry garden shows how Coleson clustered beaked yucca to screen views between the house and street.

LEFT: Coleson Bruce spent the early, at-home months of the pandemic creating his garden.

ABOVE: 'Brakelights' hesperaloe planted in a square steel pipe adds fiery color.

RIGHT: Pride of Barbados flowers all summer against a fringy backdrop of Sonoran palmetto palm.

OPPOSITE: White-flowering blackfoot daisy fills in around potted ocotillo and cactus. Citrus trees grow in a row of blue pots along the driveway.

OPPOSITE, TOP: Gray creeping germander's pink, honey-scented flowers attract a honeybee.

OPPOSITE, BOTTOM: Coleson built up one end of the streetside crevice garden with rounded boulders. Pink-flowering ruby grass emerges from a rocky nook.

ABOVE: Leaning slabs look like naturally uplifted rock in the streetside crevice garden. 'Grape Jelly' dyckia perches on top like a spiny sea urchin.

FOLLOWING PAGE: A live oak's undulating branches support a hanging chair and shade a stone table and stools.

ABOVE: Coleson rebuilt the stonework for this crevice garden more than once to get the arrangement right.

OPPOSITE, CLOCKWISE FROM TOP LEFT: Curling white threads add texture to the evergreen leaves of red yucca.

An anole extends its dewlap in a territorial display.

Wheeler's sotol bristles in a row of square steel pipes. Coleson had pipe cut to his measurements, carefully accounting for the sloping terrain and ensuring each piece was long enough to partially bury for stability.

Make a Texas-Tough Crevice Garden

Crevice gardens are popular in Colorado but relatively unknown in Texas. The traditional alpine plant palette must be jettisoned to make them work here. You can build a small-scale crevice garden in a container, or go big with an in-ground one. Study rocky outcroppings to understand how stone fits together in nature. Take inspiration from dry creek beds, canyon walls, and rocky hillsides. Here are additional tips.

» Choose a full-sun location away from litter-dropping trees and neighboring Bermudagrass lawns, to prevent runners from creeping in. Make sure your site does not hold water when it rains.

» Remove lawn and other existing plants and completely eradicate any Bermudagrass, nutgrass, or other weeds before proceeding.

» Mound a berm of lean, gravelly soil or decomposed granite and arrange flat rocks on edge, vertically or slanted in the same direction, spacing pieces about 1 inch apart. Leave bigger gaps for larger plants.

You can also use slabs of broken-up concrete paving, which keeps waste out of the landfill and saves the cost of buying stone. Bury 60 to 90 percent of the rock, filling gaps and mounding gravelly soil around the stones.

» Plant dry-loving, winter-hardy cacti, succulents, small agaves, dyckias, and groundcovers in the crevices. Buy small plants with compact root balls. Wash the soil off their roots and use chopsticks to push roots into the crevices.

Crevice Garden Plants for Central Texas

1/ **Horse crippler** (*Echinocactus texensis*): a squat, ribbed cactus with talon-like spines and showy pink, red, or orange flowers followed by fleshy red fruits. 2/ **Blackfoot daisy** (*Melampodium leucanthum*): white flowers with yellow centers seem to sparkle across this low, mounding perennial. 3/ **'Grape Jelly' dyckia** (*Dyckia* 'Grape Jelly'): deep purple, sharp-toothed leaves and orange flower spikes make this spiny little succulent a standout. 4/ **Blue daze** (*Evolvulus glomeratus*): heat-loving, mounding annual with deep blue flowers. 5/ **Narrow leaf agave** (*Agave striata*): winter-hardy, small agave with stiff, needle-like leaves and pincushion symmetry. 6/ **Ruby grass** (*Melinis nerviglumis*): pettable, rosy pink flowers and blue-green foliage, and a happy reseeder in gravel. 7/ **Mangave** (*Mangave* sp., possibly 'Kaleidoscope'): fleshy, yellow-edged leaves splattered with purple freckles. 8/ **Gopher plant** (*Euphorbia rigida*): whorled, gray-green leaves with electric-chartreuse flowering bracts in spring that feed early-foraging bees. 9/ **Gray creeping germander** (*Teucrium aroanium*): ground-hugger with lavender-pink, honey-scented flowers and gray-green leaves.

TRY-AND-TRY-AGAIN GARDEN

"MY GARDEN IS NOT AN EXAMPLE of a perfect garden," says Gina O'Hara matter-of-factly. "It's not a beautiful garden that stays beautiful. It's an example of try and try again. It's the work itself that's the joy."

An experienced green thumb with three former gardens under her belt, Gina envisioned an English-meets-Texan garden when she and husband Bill built their new home in Cedar Creek, southeast of Austin. Their nearly 7-acre lot in a rural subdivision looked like a fertile blank slate, with cedar elm, mesquite, and hackberry fringing a sunny meadow. The couple selected architect Hugh Jefferson Randolph to build a low-slung home with deep, sheltering porches, reminiscent of Gina's two inspirations: the blocky barracks of historic Fort Davis in West Texas and the veranda-shaded stone farmhouse in the movie *Out of Africa*. Next, Gina turned her attention to the garden, working with Jeff Neal Design and later Ciel Design to bring her vision to life. Low walls of stacked tumbled limestone, evocative of a timeworn western ranch, were built to define a welcoming front patio. A path of hand-pressed Mexican brick and limestone leads around the L-shaped house through a series of garden rooms, including a round "eye" and semicircular "eyebrow" garden.

Gina was delighted with the structure of her new garden. To her frustration, however, the plants failed to thrive, remaining stunted in a way she'd never experienced with her former gardens, or they died outright. After several years with little growth to show for it, she brought in landscape architecture firm Shademaker Studio to solve the problem. Soil-core samples revealed an impervious layer of clay holding water like a rubber pond liner beneath the planting beds. Even when the soil felt dry to the touch, plants were drowning at the roots, and the clay thwarted root growth. "Big Lindheimer's muhly grasses that had been in the ground for ten years, we thought when we dug them up there was going to be a big root system," Gina recalls. "But the roots had not grown 4 inches. They were basically sitting on top of the clay."

Working with Shademaker, Gina had the garden beds excavated to a depth of 18 inches and refilled and mounded with 75 yards of good soil. New plants were planted in early 2023, just a few months before a summer-long record heat wave arrived. Municipal watering restrictions on aboveground irrigation soon became a moratorium. That spurred Gina to install efficient (and unrestricted) drip irrigation and three large cisterns to collect rainwater off her roof. Through all the ups and downs and weather extremes, Gina's gardening helper, Martin Beltran Flores, has been invaluable in keeping the garden going. "I could not have this garden without his help," she says.

With its flowering perennials and seed-

OPPOSITE: 'White Cloud' is an ivory-flowering cultivar of the popular rosy pink Gulf muhly grass.

FOLLOWING PAGE: Grasses and perennials fill a semicircular "eyebrow" bed that arches around a round "eye" of red gomphrena.

Gina O'Hara, pictured with Ginger, her poodle, presses on whenever a new gardening challenge arises.

bearing grasses, the garden attracts a lot of butterflies and birds. Gina views tending her garden as a stewardship of wildlife. "Supporting the bees, birds, and butterflies is a big part of what this garden is about," she says. Gina is particularly fond of her cutting garden, where she feels free to try out any plant that catches her eye. Set away from the house and fenced to keep out deer, the cutting garden gives a lot and asks little. "If you want to do something and are limited on space, money, or time," she says, "do a raised-bed cutting garden. You can make the beds yourself from cedar. There's no pressure for it to look right. I just allow myself to see a pretty plant and take it home. It's a fun garden."

When she's not tending her garden, Gina enjoys sitting with Bill and their standard poodle, Ginger, on the shady back porch. It's a quiet spot, good for thinking. "I've always been in search of my passion," Gina muses. "I've tried the cello twice. I've taken pottery. I worked with a trapeze coach for three years. I've always been looking for the thing that would be my passion. And all the time, I'm gardening. Finally I realized, it's this! This is my passion. I've gardened so long it's part of my being, part of my day. I just hadn't owned it. I am a gardener."

ABOVE: A tumbled limestone wall designed to evoke an old, falling-down West Texas ranch encloses a patio garden at the front door. 'Little Gem' magnolia, 'White Cloud' Gulf muhly, and white lantana offer a white-garden welcome.

LEFT: Circular beds along the front of the house add depth and interest.

ABOVE LEFT: Passionflower vine smothers the cutting garden fence.

LEFT: An avid antique hunter, Gina designed her red-trimmed garden shed around an old door she found in a Gonzales antique shop.

ABOVE: A white garden glowing with 'Feathertop' pennisetum and annual gomphrena is enclosed by a wall of dark gray brick.

ABOVE: Gina found her faux bois table and chairs at an antique shop. Faux bois is concrete crafted to look like wood, usually made into furniture or planters.

OPPOSITE, CLOCKWISE FROM TOP LEFT: Possumhaw holly berries ripen in fall to feed birds through winter.

Thai basil's purple flowers and stems harmonize with the gray brick of the garden wall.

Ginger lounges on a daybed on the cool, shady porch.

Add Seating Out Front

Backyard patios and decks are nice when you crave seclusion. But a front-yard sitting area provides an opportunity for socializing with neighbors or watching the world go by. Just by virtue of making room for a couple of chairs, a front patio creates a more welcoming entry for your home. And it transforms a front yard from a merely decorative space into a functional one.

» Before starting, check homeowners' association (HOA) rules, if you have one, to make sure a front seating area is allowed.

» Remove lawn to make room for a patio near the front door or perhaps under a shady tree. A bonus: adding a front patio means you'll have less turf to mow and water.

» Paving can be as simple as gravel, flagstone, pavers, or even wood mulch, which looks most natural under a tree's broad canopy.

» Add comfortable chairs and a low table for lounging and neighborly visits. Or place a picnic table or outdoor dining set, and take the office outside on a nice afternoon. A patio umbrella is useful for as-needed shade.

» Create a feeling of enclosure by constructing a low wall or open-style fence between the patio and street. Size it under 3 feet tall to preserve sightlines to the street. A low hedge or clusters of medium-sized grasses can accomplish a similar effect.

» Include outdoor lighting so your patio is useable in the evening and to enhance the welcoming atmosphere.

Cutting Garden Flowers for Central Texas

1/ Wheat celosia (*Celosia spicata*): hot-weather annual with magenta flower spikes in fall. This particular plant shows fasciation, an abnormal but typically harmless growth pattern.
2/ Maximilian sunflower (*Helianthus maximiliani*): native prairie perennial with yellow flowers in late summer and fall along 4- to 6-foot stems. **3/ Butterfly vine** (*Mascagnia macroptera*): evergreen vine with lemon-yellow flowers in late summer, which turn into butterfly-shaped seedpods—an unusual addition to bouquets. **4 & 5/ Gomphrena** (*Gomphrena globosa*): round, clover-like blossoms in summer and fall, in colors ranging from white to pink, purple, and red. 'Fireworks' is a taller cultivar with tufted, hot-pink flowers. **6/ Ruby grass** (*Melinis nerviglumis*): soft, rosy pink flowers on slender stems make a textural addition to cut-flower arrangements.

POCKET PRAIRIE
IN THE CITY

JOHN HART ASHER WAS entertaining friends at home one evening, not long after planting a prairie garden in his backyard. "I'll never forget it," he says. "That night there was an eruption of light from the landscape. It was emanating from my yard. None of the other yards had it. There hadn't ever been lightning bugs here, but now there were." John Hart's elation increased with each new species that showed up in his garden. Screech owls, black-bellied whistling ducks, painted buntings, yellow warblers, Mississippi kites, rough green snakes, toads, lizards, skinks, and insects of all kinds appeared, finding shelter or sustenance where once a tangle of Bermudagrass and pigweed grew. "That was my indicator of success, critters coming in that I hadn't seen before," he says.

What draws such a rich diversity of wildlife to this ⅓-acre plot just 3 miles from downtown Austin is a meadowy mix of native grasses, perennials, and annuals—a microcosm of the Blackland Prairie that once sustained bison and other wild creatures from the Texas-Oklahoma border down to San Antonio. Today, less than 1 percent of the prairie remains. Most of that belt of fertile soil was converted long ago into farmland—and nowadays into housing and commercial developments. As a passionate advocate for native plants and a principal of Blackland Collaborative, an ecology-based consulting group, John Hart was eager to restore a bit of Texas prairie in his own backyard. "I call it a pocket prairie," he says. "It's an offering to other species, to allow them

space where they've been pushed out. It's a chance to support diversity."

John Hart purchased his east Austin property in 2007, attracted by its deep lot and the possibilities for making a prairie garden. A small house on the lot served for a while. But eventually he and wife Bonnie Evridge rebuilt to suit the needs of their growing family, which includes two young sons, nine-year-old Adler and five-year-old Fen. As the boys have grown, the garden has provided a place for them to engage with nature, exploring for bugs, snakes, and butterflies and helping their dad seed and plant. "I want them to help in order to know that they have helped, if even in a small way, to save the world," says John Hart. "I want them to know that action results in impact, and even though there are many challenges before us, their efforts matter." With this kind of garden, there's no worry about the occasional soccer ball bouncing through. Prairies are disturbance-driven ecosystems after all, he points out. They evolved to thrive under the trampling of a bison's hooves and to rebound after wildfire. Prairie gardeners must therefore "be the bison," says John Hart, willing to dig and cut back to create the disturbance that such plants appreciate.

John Hart grew up in Mississippi, and as a teen he worked on a 600-acre wildlife farm,

OPPOSITE: Purple-flowering horsemint offers lemon-scented foliage by the swimming pool.

FOLLOWING PAGE: A round, concrete-edged pond adds a contemporary accent against the shaggy prairie garden.

planting soybeans and other crops to create food plots for hunting. "That planted the seed in me about gardening for wildlife," he says. He moved to Austin in 2004 to get a master's degree in landscape architecture from the University of Texas. When he started making his own garden, he quickly learned that gardening in Texas is challenging. "In Mississippi you have a lot of rain," he says. "You stick something in the ground, and it'll grow. Texas is a really hard environment to garden in. And with climate change, it's going to become even more challenging, with more droughts and deluges." Growing native grassland plants improves the odds of success, he points out, because they evolved to withstand such extremes. "Texas has always been a hot place with frequent droughts," he says. "That's why the prairie is here. Prairies evolved as a direct response to a lack of precipitation." Prairie grasses send roots deep into the soil, searching out moisture far below the surface. If they can't find it, they simply go dormant and wait for rain to return. And while back-to-back deep freezes in 2021 and 2022 took a toll on native trees and shrubs, native grasses and perennials bounced right back. "With climate change," says John Hart, "people say, 'Plant trees, plant trees, plant trees.' That's one of the worst things you can do in a grassland biome. One, grasslands are extremely threatened. And two, they lock up tons of carbon, about 1.6 metric tons of carbon per acre per year. While trees might be better at carbon sequestration, they store it in aboveground biomass. And when a tree dies, it releases all that carbon. Prairies and grasses lock carbon in the ground. As long as you don't till it up, you've locked it away."

During the pandemic, John Hart and Bonnie added a swimming pool for their family's enjoyment, and a patch of St. Augustine lawn near the house remains for the boys to kick a soccer ball around. "It's not like I've given over the entire landscape to prairie plants," says John Hart, "but I've made as much space as possible." He's been experimenting with a native lawn around the pool, starting out with buffalograss sod. When that turned patchy, he filled in with short native grasses like Texas grama, curly mesquite, slender grama, and blue grama. "I'm recreating a shortgrass prairie," he says. Along the fences, he grows a diversity of native flowering perennials, including Gregg's salvia, mealy blue sage, plateau goldeneye, big bluestem, big muhly, frostweed, and Turk's cap. Native vines—alamo vine, crossvine, coral honeysuckle, and Carolina jessamine—are encouraged to clamber up a steel trellis over a patio for shade, seasonal color, and fragrance, as well as sustenance for pollinators of all kinds.

"So go the insects, so goes us," says John Hart. "Making space for all these other species, it's not entirely altruistic. It's for our survival as well. Doug Tallamy says, in his book *Nature's Best Hope*, do whatever you can. If you can convert a third of your land, do it. If you can't do that much, do what you can. Collectively, if everyone's adding some habitat, it's going to have a massive impact." John Hart's garden is an oasis beckoning to birds and other wildlife. Each spring, magenta winecups and pink evening primrose ramble along his boardwalk path, offering chalices of nectar for butterflies and bees. Graceful stems of eastern gamagrass bend under the weight of fringy orange flowers dangling like fish on a line; the foliage feeds the caterpillars of several species of butterflies and moths. Purple, pagoda-tiered flowers of horsemint draw butterflies and hummingbirds eager to fuel up on nectar. Wands of mealy blue sage entice bumblebees to join the pollinator buffet. John Hart surveys the scene with delight. "Even in a small garden," he says, "you're going to see amazing things happen. A pocket prairie is an entire universe at your feet, if you take the time to look."

ABOVE: Mealy blue sage and hot-pink autumn sage border a native lawn of buffalograss, grama grasses, and curly mesquite.

LEFT: John Hart Asher cradles one of his chickens in front of an abstract steel design on the shed door.

ABOVE: Tall stems of eastern gamagrass show off orange flowers in spring.

RIGHT: An airy, triangular arbor frames a patio by the pool. John Hart is training several vines up it for shade.

OPPOSITE: A boardwalk path bisects the prairie garden, offering an elevated view and connecting the house with the swimming pool, chicken coop, and shed.

ABOVE LEFT: Pink evening primrose brightens the streetside garden.

LEFT: A cistern stores 3000 gallons of rainwater "para el jardín" (which translates to "for the garden") collected from the house roof.

ABOVE: The front garden blazes with color in spring thanks to retama, winecup, black-eyed Susan, and pink evening primrose, with a Wheeler's sotol for evergreen structure. The front door offers its own colorful welcome.

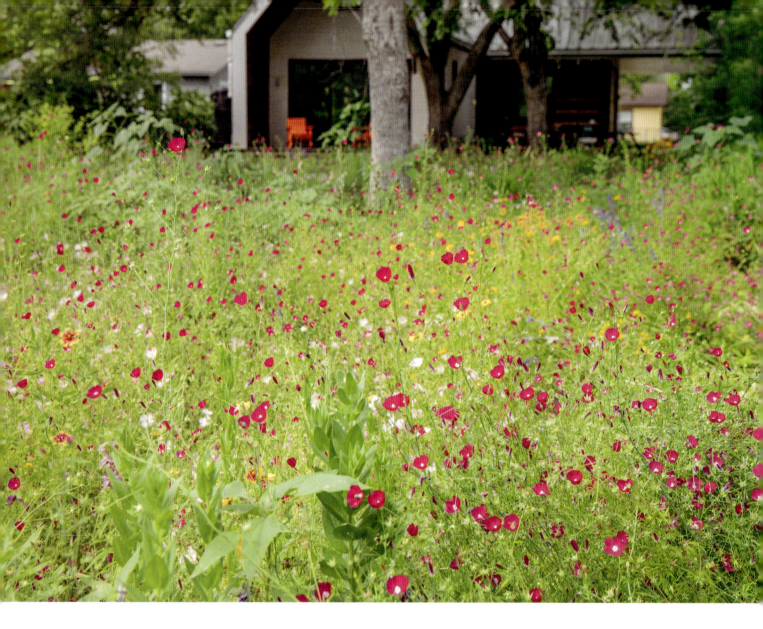

ABOVE: Standing winecup's magenta chalices stand out in the spring prairie garden.

OPPOSITE, CLOCKWISE FROM TOP:
The pocket prairie makes a naturalistic backdrop for the swimming pool and arbor-framed patio.

Stone pavers in the native lawn give lounge chairs a secure footing.

Ladybugs and their orange-striped larvae feast on aphids on a frostweed leaf. John Hart doesn't fret about insect damage, knowing their natural predators will show up too.

Plant a Pocket Prairie

The great prairies of the Southern Plains were tilled under long ago. But if you grow even a handful of native prairie plants, you can provide a pocket-sized oasis for pollinators, birds, lizards, and other wild creatures. Every yard with a pocket prairie contributes habitat, and it adds up. Here are tips for making your own.

» Choose a spot with at least a half day of full sun, and ideally all-day sun.

» Take your time eradicating turfgrass and weeds. If you have Bermudagrass or zoysia, solarize with clear or black plastic all spring, summer, and fall to kill as much of the vegetation as possible. Follow up with an application of herbicide if necessary. If you have St. Augustine turf, it's easier to remove. Dig it up by hand or use a sod cutter. Do not plant or sow seed until you're certain all turfgrass and weeds have been eradicated.

» Rake out dead foliage, but do not till, which can stir up dormant weed seeds in the soil.

» Decide which native prairie species to plant, based on your soil conditions (sticky clay, sandy, rocky? moist or dry?). Select around 50 percent grasses and 50 percent forbs (flowering herbaceous plants). Shop for plants at local nurseries specializing in natives, online native seed suppliers, and Native Plant Society of Texas plant sales.

» In the fall, sow wildflower seeds when rain is in the forecast. Walk across the soil after sowing to lightly press seeds in. Then plant potted grasses and forbs. If you can't find everything you want for a fall planting, add more in early spring.

» Water well and keep new plants moist but not wet. Do not fertilize. Prairie plants don't need it.

» As your pocket prairie grows, watch for weeds and promptly pull them. Avoid pesticides, including mosquito spraying, as they kill pollinators too.

» Watch wildlife flock to your garden!

Prairie Garden Plants for Central Texas

1/ **Wild bergamot** (*Monarda fistulosa*): shaggy pompom flowers on tall stems attract butterflies and hummingbirds from late spring into summer. 2/ **Texas prairie parsley** (*Polytaenia texana*): clusters of yellow flowers like fireworks, a biennial nectar plant for butterflies and host plant for black swallowtails. 3/ **Shrubby copperleaf** (*Acalypha phleoides*): low-growing perennial with coppery bottlebrush flowers. 4/ **Eastern gamagrass** (*Tripsacum dactyloides*): tall perennial with orange, dangling flowers and sharp-edged leaves. 5/ **Lindheimer's muhly** (*Muhlenbergia lindheimeri*): fine-textured, upright, blue-green leaves and silvery seedheads in fall. 6/ **Giant coneflower** (*Rudbeckia maxima*): blue-green leaves and towering flower stalks with brown cones and skirts of golden petals. 7/ **Mealy blue sage** (*Salvia farinacea*): tall stems topped with blue flower spikes, attractive to bees and butterflies. 8/ **Antelope horns milkweed** (*Asclepias asperula*): spherical, green-and-white flower clusters attract bees and butterflies, including monarchs, whose larvae feed only on milkweed. 9/ **Little bluestem** (*Schizachyrium scoparium*): small grass with blue-green foliage that turns reddish bronze in fall.

A SENTIMENTAL GARDEN

IF EVERY GARDEN is a form of autobiography, as the saying goes, then Jackson Broussard's garden is a deeply personal memoir. Happy memories unspool from treasured keepsakes he's embedded in walls and paths, built into gates and arbors, and artfully arranged on tables and shelves. A pair of faded-red toy cars cemented into a scrap-stone pedestal evokes days of boyhood play. An old firehose nozzle, acquired in college and squirreled away for years, has new purpose as a fountain in a fishpond. Rollers sourced from Mr. Grind's butcher shop ("they had the best sausage in five counties," swears Jackson) slide a custom gate along its frame. His grandfather's stash of rebar supports a pear arbor that Jackson pleached over a path. "My little garden is sentimental," he admits. "I've got bricks from my best friend's house, stones that remind me of my grandfather, plants that friends gave me. Seeing those things makes me happy, more than just seeing something that's beautiful."

Jackson, a garden designer and co-owner of JPB Design Studio, grew up in his gray-green east Austin bungalow, and he's sentimental about the house too. As a kid he'd climb on the roof and watch airplanes thunder into the sky at the old airport (since demolished) behind the house. Later on, his parents rented out the house, and from time to time he'd help his dad make repairs. When his folks offered to sell it to him, Jackson jumped at the chance. After living in the bungalow for a few years, he built a two-story ADU (accessory dwelling unit) in the backyard as his main residence and began leasing out the bungalow. "Once I built the back house," he says, "that's when the garden took off."

The garden boldly reaches out to the street via an arch of four Bradford pears interlaced on a rebar frame above a limestone walk. "The pear arbor is a big focal point," explains Jackson, "but it's also capturing the sight line from the street to the front door, and it's leading you." At each tree trunk, a rectangular pedestal of scrap stone, brick, and tile—even a New Orleans water-meter cover—adds a rustic-modern architectural accent. In the center of the walk, a cross-axis view of a basalt birdbath on one side and a deer sculpture on the other relieves the tunnel-like effect, encouraging a look around. "There are little things hidden to the left and the right," says Jackson, "and that discovery is fun for me and other people. Not everybody gets that sort of thing, and a lot of people breeze right by. But the people that are detail oriented, they get it, and those are the people I really connect with."

A small front patio screened by a smoke tree, firebush, and clipped boxwood gives Jackson's tenants a place to relax outdoors. They can also hang out at the biergarten table in the open-sided carport. "It always has a breeze," says Jackson, "even at two o'clock in the middle of summer." The backyard is Jackson's private domain. A pair of tall pillars, one partly clad in scrap stone, topped with ruffle-rimmed urns, marks the way to his front door. Arranged along a low wall, dozens of succulents in terracotta pots make up

OPPOSITE: A pleached arbor of four Bradford pears makes a shady tunnel along the front walk, accented with low pedestals of stone, brick, and mementos that Jackson collected over the years.

FOLLOWING PAGE: The angular geometry of Jackson's back garden is especially apparent from an upper-story window.

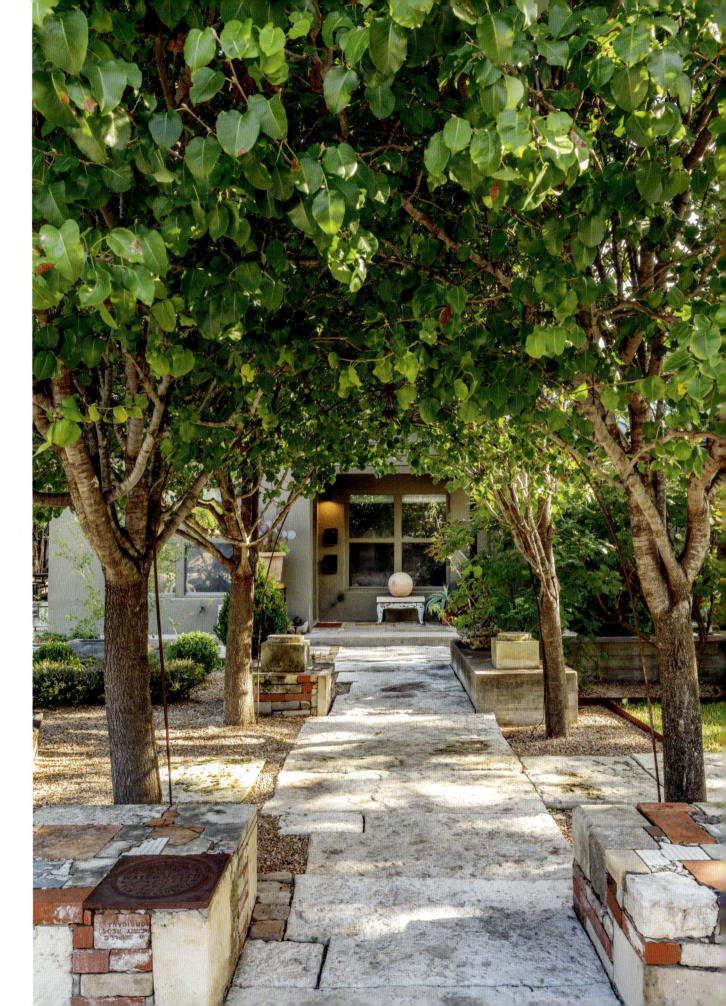

what Jackson calls his plant altar. "You can't see my door when you're walking up," he says. "That's the reason for the columns and plant altar—to make it feel important enough to go to the front door. It also sets up a sight line." A sliding gate of welded rebar opens to his backyard garden, where a triangular lawn and deck laid on the diagonal draw the eye along the longest axis of the narrow, rectangular space, making it feel bigger than it really is. "Some people walk onto the deck because they want to see everything," says Jackson. "Other people walk onto the lawn to look at the plants. I go sit on the swing. I can sit on the swing and see just about everything."

At one end of the deck, a board-formed concrete cube contains a round fishpond—"I love to play with geometry," says Jackson—that doubles as extra seating during parties. "That way I don't need as much furniture," he says. "When the weather is nice, I open the back door and can hear the fountain in the house." Patio chairs surround a steel-ring firepit, where he likes to cook over an open flame in a Dutch oven and make s'mores with his nieces. A stone tabletop converts the firepit into a coffee table "for the 350 days of the year that you don't need a fire in Austin," jokes Jackson. Nearby, a wood-burning grill gives him more outdoor cooking options. An angled steel arbor visually divides the patio from the lawn. Atop the arbor, Jackson attached an old school bell that has special significance for his family. "The bell came from an old elementary school in Seguin called Weinert Elementary," he says. "My grandmother went to Weinert. My mom went to Weinert. In theory, my mom and grandmother both rang that bell when they were kids. Since then, my sister has rung the bell, and both my nieces have rung the bell. So that's four generations of women in my life that have rung that bell."

Despite his sentimental attachments, Jackson has learned to let things go when necessary, particularly plants that haven't held up to volatile weather swings in recent years. "The big freeze in 2021 killed a lot of plants," he says. "I'd always looked at gardens as, they're going to get better as they age. Well, with climate change, that may not always hold true. The last eight summers have been the hottest on record, or something along those lines. And we've had big freezes. We're asking plants to handle 115°F down to 5°F. That's difficult." After Winter Storm Uri killed a screening hedge of bay laurel, Jackson replaced it with cold-tolerant 'Nellie R. Stevens' holly. With other plants, he's watching to see how well they recover after deep freezes and weighing which ones are worth replanting. "It's a time decision and a monetary decision," he says. "You can't keep putting your hand in the fire. I'm not planting olives anymore. I'm planting desert willows instead. And there are a lot of old-school plants like cleyera that work well and have been in the nursery biz for 75 years for a reason. Everything doesn't have to be a crazy, exotic plant. Experiment, but don't play with your entire yard."

For Jackson, a garden is about more than just plants, as much as he enjoys them. It's about lifestyle. Years ago, as a college student studying abroad, he lived for a time in Tuscany. The experience was transformative. "Italy was like fireworks going off in my brain," he recalls. "I studied Italian gardens, Italian furniture, woodworking, stone carving. The lifestyle, the attention to food, not being in a rat race, siesta, family time, enjoying your life—that trip changed my life." Italy informed his ideas of what a garden should be: a place to putter, relax with family and friends, cook, and just enjoy being outdoors. "My place is about 50 percent plants and 50 percent hardscape," he says. "I don't want just hardscape that's nasty-hot all the time. But I don't want it to be just a jungle of plants I have to take care of all the time either, because I like to do other things. I like to grill. I like to sit by the fire and roast marshmallows with my nieces. I like my hammock. I like my water feature. I love my swing. I want to enjoy my garden."

ABOVE: A shady, breezy carport serves as a workshop for Jackson and hangout space for his tenants.

LEFT: Jackson Broussard integrates objects that hold personal significance into his garden.

ABOVE: Pillars of board-formed concrete, one partially faced with stone and brick, and Jackson's plant altar draw visitors toward the hidden front door of his backyard house.

RIGHT: A steel arbor topped with an old school bell frames a swinging bench, Jackson's favorite spot to sit, and a rooster sculpture at the end of the lawn.

OPPOSITE: The violet pads of 'Santa Rita' prickly pear look sculptural against a sunlit stucco wall.

ABOVE: A firehose-nozzle fountain pours a smooth stream of water into a circular pond inset in a concrete cube.

ABOVE RIGHT: Jackson welded rebar to make a sliding gate on rollers salvaged from an old butcher shop.

OPPOSITE, CLOCKWISE FROM TOP:
Collected metal and stone objects are artfully displayed on a workbench.

Toy cars from Jackson's childhood are mortared into a pedestal along the front walk, offering a moment of discovery for curious visitors.

A mockingbird alights on a basalt bird-bath for a drink.

ABOVE: A patio table does double duty as a firepit when the stone lid is removed.

OPPOSITE, CLOCKWISE FROM TOP: A low wall, bushy plants, and an umbrella screen an intimate front-yard patio from view of the street.

Slabs of limestone and bricks make a collected path to the door of the front house.

A collection of succulents, cacti, and a large blue nolina are unified by Italian terracotta on Jackson's plant altar.

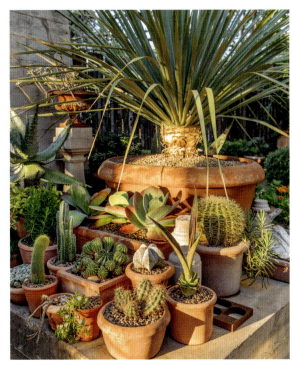

Express Yourself in the Garden

Add personality to your garden and conjure happy memories by incorporating sentimental keepsakes or collections. If you don't have a supply of memory-making relics on hand, you can repurpose thrift-store or yard-sale finds to foster moments of discovery. Here are some ideas.

» Turn old ironwork into a trellis or gate, or hang it on a wall as decoration. Jackson repurposed a piece of decorative ironwork for a gated opening to his outdoor shower.

» Mortar small objects—durable toys, interesting rocks, ceramic pottery—into a stone wall. Or display them on a shelf or bench—or atop an arbor, like Jackson's schoolhouse bell. Make sure objects drain water to avoid creating mosquito-breeding puddles.

» Reimagine salvaged materials. Jackson assembled sections of metal pipe into a birdhouse atop a tall post.

» Turn any object that can hold soil into a planter. If you can drill or hammer a drainage hole or two, it'll work: a toy dump truck, metal trash bin, teapot, colander (lined with landscape fabric to keep soil from washing out), birdcage, a pair of old boots. It may not last forever, but it's a clever way to upcycle an object that might otherwise collect dust in the attic.

» Use a collection of shells or rocks as topper mulch for a potted plant. Every time you see them, you'll be reminded of a favorite place or the period of time when you collected them.

Summer-Tough Plants for Containers

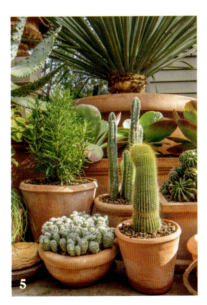

1/ Gulf muhly (*Muhlenbergia capillaris*): showy pink flowers in autumn resemble cotton candy, held above fine-textured green leaves. **2/ Giant leopard plant** (*Farfugium japonicum* var. *giganteum*) and **purple heart** (*Tradescantia pallida*): Leopard plant has round, glossy leaves, needs regular water. Purple heart thrives on neglect, has rich-purple foliage and violet flowers. **3/ Blue nolina** (*Nolina nelsonii*): strappy blue-green leaves on a slowly trunking plant. Must be protected from severe freezes, or try Wheeler's sotol instead. **4/ Ghost plant** (*Graptopetalum paraguayense*): fleshy succulent with pinkish gray rosettes that spread and cascade on long stems. **5/ Cactus species:** small cacti like mammillaria make excellent potted plants in Texas summers, but protect them from freezes in winter. **6/ Fire sticks** (*Euphorbia tirucalli* 'Sticks on Fire'): vertical, branching stems turn coral in full sun and when drought stressed. Protect from freezes.

HARVESTING
THE RAIN

"I HAVEN'T COUNTED my trees, but I have a ton, mostly live oaks, and they've been here a long time," says Janie Orr of her half-acre wooded lot in Austin. "I knew the trees would be king. They would set the script, and we would write the lines." She and her late husband, John, wrote those lines of their garden design with the professional expertise of their daughter Jennifer Orr, a landscape architect and co-founder of Studio Balcones, an Austin-based landscape architecture firm specializing in ecologically sensitive sites.

The property and its trees were a lucky find. Janie and John had been searching for a home in Central Austin when they found a 1940s ranch overlooking Waller Creek under a canopy of heritage trees. "We couldn't believe you could feel like you lived in the country, but you didn't," recalls Janie. To make the house livable, the couple had to tear it down to the foundation and rebuild. Designed by architect Emily Little, the sage green stucco home nestles among the trees, partly hidden from the street.

As Jennifer worked with her parents on the garden's design, they faced several challenges: compacted soil; runoff and erosion on the sloping site; and the puzzle of how to construct a driveway (the old house didn't have one) without harming the trees. "Everywhere you turned, you had a heritage tree," says Jennifer. "One tree was 42 inches in diameter—a serious root zone. Arborist Michael Embesi worked with us to figure out a driveway that wouldn't be so hard on the tree roots." To avoid over-paving

and allow water and air to reach the roots, Jennifer designed a semi-porous driveway with alternating bands of concrete and decomposed granite mixed with a pathway stabilizer. The strikingly stripey paving leads to the carport and flows along the porch to the front door, making a courtyard-like transition between house and garden.

Using flat limestone boulders, Jennifer built check dams—low-profile barriers laid lengthwise along the slope—to address erosion under the trees. The dams slow runoff when it rains, giving water time to soak into the soil and preventing soil-nourishing leaf litter and mulch from washing away. As a bonus, the dams double as narrow maintenance paths through the plants. Under the trees, Jennifer planted masses of shade-tolerant natives like inland sea oats, American beautyberry, Turk's cap, white mistflower, river fern, twistleaf yucca, heartleaf skullcap, and columbine. "These don't need much water to look good, even in a hot, dry summer," she says. Spring-flowering understory trees, mostly Mexican plum and Texas redbud, were clustered at the top of the stairs near the street to fill out the mid-level and block car headlights coming down the hill. More sun along the street allows red yucca and

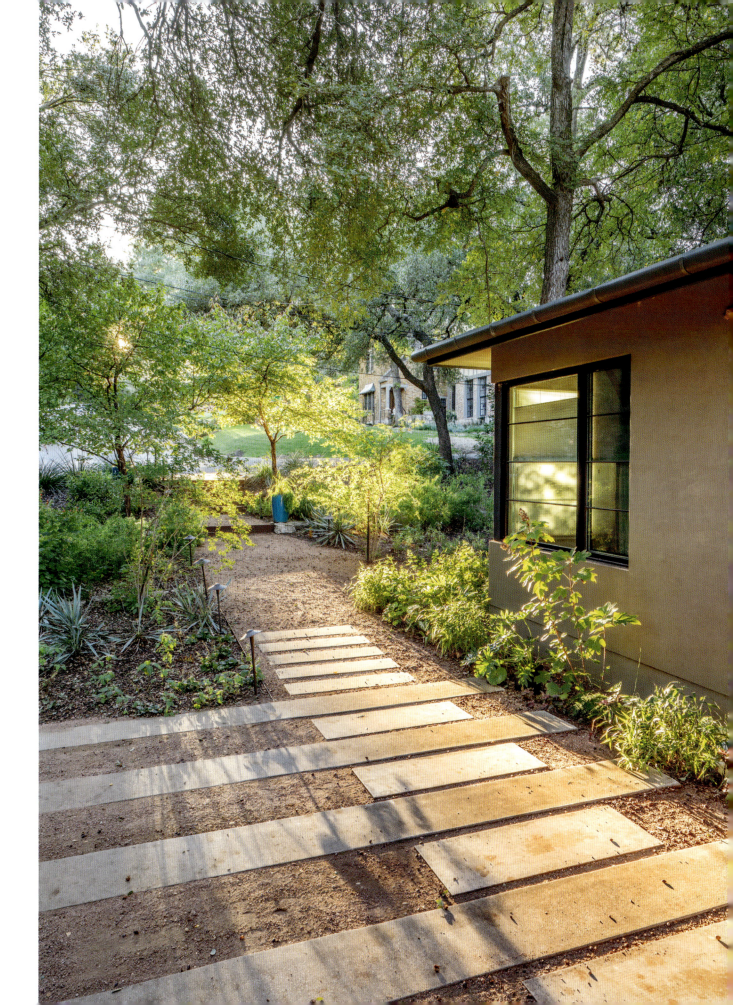

firecracker fern to flourish. "It feels secluded," says Janie. "I enjoy the fact that I can watch all the dog walkers without feeling exposed."

To loosely enclose a small deck by a front bedroom, Jennifer built gabion planter walls in an L shape and filled them with evergreen holly fern. "Because of the tree roots, you can't have anything with a foundation," says Janie. "So gabion boxes were about the only option." In the backyard, a screened porch and deck overlook a zoysia lawn where Janie's seven grandchildren play soccer and other games. Along one side, in a natural bowl, Jennifer terraced the lawn with metal risers and a railing to create a small amphitheater. A family wedding, children's birthday parties, and musical performances have brought together three generations of Orrs and their friends. When it's just her, Janie enjoys sitting on the back porch and birdwatching. "I have a wren family that never leaves and robins, blue jays, and cardinals," she says.

Jennifer talked her parents into installing a robust water-harvesting system that includes two industrial-grade, inflatable water bladders hidden under the porch and a galvanized cistern in the backyard. "The bladders hold about 10,000 gallons," says Jennifer, "and the cistern holds 2500 or 3000 gallons. They're all connected, and the gutters fill them up." Janie runs her irrigation system using harvested rainwater for much of the year, although it usually runs dry around July. When that happens, city water fills the cistern so the irrigation can run. "That means you never disconnect the system," says Jennifer. The important thing, she adds, is to have enough water-storage capacity to make the whole setup worthwhile. "Most people, when they do rainwater harvesting, they don't do it big enough," she explains. "We wanted to get to 15,000 gallons, and we got pretty close. It's all about economy of scale. If you're going to invest in the gutters and backflow preventer and pump, but you can't use it enough because you don't have enough storage, it's not going to save you much money."

Along with the benefits of rainwater harvesting, a plant palette that's 95 percent native, and trees for shade, Janie draws on years of experience as a Texas gardener to cope with extreme-weather events like deep freezes, heat waves, drought, and deluges that make the creek creep up the lawn. "It's tricky," says Janie. "You think you've got it all figured out, and then you get surprised." For example, after severe freezes in 2021 and 2022, the redbuds along the street died. "Who'd have ever thought you'd lose redbuds?" she says. The biggest lesson she's learned, after nine years of tending the garden, is that even a well-planned and eco-friendly garden requires regular care. "When you have a smart designer and excellent contractor and state-of-the-art watering system, you think that everything is going to sing and you won't have to do a lot, but that's not true. You still have to tend the garden. You cannot have a garden in absentia. Someone has to love it."

And love it she does. "The garden calls me," says Janie. "I think there's nothing better than pulling weeds or taming part of the woods, especially in spring. I don't ever read books or go anywhere in the spring because I'd much rather be here."

ABOVE: An arching bloom spike of red yucca adds color and draws hummingbirds.

LEFT: Janie Orr and her daughter Jennifer Orr, a landscape architect, collaborated on the design of the garden.

OPPOSITE: A scrim of native perennials buffers the house from the street and offers views of flowers and wildlife activity when Janie looks out her windows.

ABOVE: A galvanized cistern stores around 2500 gallons of rainwater collected from the house roof.

RIGHT: Gabion walls don't require an excavated and poured foundation, which could have harmed the roots of established trees. A layer of soil in the walls supports holly ferns.

ABOVE: A screened porch overlooks the backyard lawn and an amphitheater built into a natural bowl, where many Orr family celebrations have taken place.

RIGHT: The seedheads of inland sea oats, a shade-tolerant grass, dangle like fish on a line.

Catch the Rain

Rainwater in much of Texas is too precious to let it wash away into storm drains. Use passive and active rainwater collection to hold onto every drop.

» **RAIN BARRELS AND CISTERNS** Place a rain barrel under a downspout to collect runoff from your roof. Connect multiple barrels together for more capacity, or go even bigger with a large poly or galvanized cistern. Small tanks are useful for filling watering cans for hand watering. Bigger tanks require a pump for effective use and can be attached to a watering hose. With careful planning, they can even be connected, like Janie's, to an automatic irrigation system.

» **BLADDER TANKS** These low-profile collapsible tanks, which inflate as they fill with water, fit under a deck or porch or even under the house. Hidden out of sight, they preserve your yard for plants and living space.

» **CHECK DAMS** To slow runoff on a gently sloping lot, build a low barrier of heavy rock lengthwise across the slope. By slowing runoff, a check dam gives soil more time to absorb rainwater.

» **TERRACING** For a steeper slope, use terracing to create flatter planting beds, which are better able to hold rainwater and resist erosion.

» **RAIN GARDENS** A rain garden, planted in a shallow depression, captures runoff and holds it, allowing it to recharge the soil. Plants in a rain garden also help cleanse runoff of pollutants.

» **PERMEABLE PAVING** Choose paving options that allow rainwater to reach tree roots, like gravel, decomposed granite (DG), and unmortared flagstone or pavers. Avoid the use of weed-barrier fabric under gravel or DG, as it compromises permeability.

» **MORE PLANTS, LESS PAVING** Groundcovers and other soil-holding plants help to slow runoff and soak up rainwater. Mulch helps too, but avoid the temptation to pile it on, as a too-thick layer can prevent rainwater from reaching the soil and thirsty roots. All that's needed is 2 to 3 inches.

Native Plants for Dry Shade in Central Texas

1/ **Yaupon holly** (*Ilex vomitoria*): evergreen small tree with red berries in fall and winter, a favorite of birds. 2/ **Inland sea oats** (*Chasmanthium latifolium*): shade-loving grass with flat, drooping seedheads that start bright green and ripen to tan. It seeds out readily and makes a good choice for erosion control. 3/ **Turk's cap** (*Malvaviscus arboreus* var. *drummondii*): woody shrub with bright red spiraling flowers that bloom spring through fall, with small red fruits in fall. 4/ **American** **beautyberry** (*Callicarpa americana*): medium to large shrub with arching branches that bear clusters of glossy purple berries in fall, which birds love. 5/ **White mistflower** (*Ageratina havanensis*): branching shrub with fragrant clusters of fuzzy white flowers in fall, which attract bees and butterflies. 6/ **Pale-leaf yucca** (*Yucca pallida*): powder blue, spine-tipped leaves with a tall white flower spike in spring. For dry shade or sun.

THE AUTHOR'S HOME GROUND

LIKE MANY PEOPLE who've relocated to Texas, when I started gardening I looked first to familiar plants from my former home region, the Carolinas. That's how I ended up buying azaleas in Austin. Even the tactful advice of a salesperson at the local nursery didn't dissuade me (after all, they were selling them!). I planted my row of white azaleas, kept them watered, and waited with anticipation. The little shrubs endured the long, hot summer but sulkily refused to grow. In spring, the masses of flowers I expected didn't materialize either. It went on like this for a few disappointing years until I finally conceded. I dug up the ill-suited azaleas and planted something else.

Since then, through three decades of gardening in Austin, I've made plenty of other mistakes. But I've also learned a couple of things worth passing along. First, plant what wants to live here (or wherever *you* are). For me, that includes native plants and well-adapted nonnatives that take in stride the heat and humidity, thin limestone or sticky clay soil, and drought-flood-drought cycle that Central Texas is known for. Second, it's a fact that every gardener kills lots of plants, so don't let dead plants discourage you. Plant more of what succeeds, discard what doesn't, and just keep planting. Gardening is an act of optimism and experimentation, and it rewards doggedness.

I'm on my third Austin garden now, a live oak–shaded, deer-infested, limestone-riddled, ⅓-acre lot at the edge of a forested canyon. The dry shade,

the deer, the rock, the slope—all of that was novel to me when I began this garden in 2008. The property, mostly level in front, drops off steeply in back. A backyard fence keeps out the deer and most of the rabbits and armadillos, but out front it's like a petting zoo—without the petting. Accordingly, I've whittled the plant palette in front to deer-resistant grasses and sedges, fibrous yuccas and sotols, fragrant-leaved salvias and herbs, and fuzzy foliage plants like Jerusalem sage and heartleaf skullcap. In the fenced back garden, deer can't get at anything, which allows for more variety, but the shade from a dozen live oaks still nudges the garden toward foliage texture rather than colorful flowers.

Many visits to the Lady Bird Johnson Wildflower Center, Austin's native plant botanical garden, fostered in me a deep appreciation for Texas flora—not just their hardiness but their rugged beauty. Approximately 60 percent of the species I'm growing are Texas natives. They provide habitat for wild creatures like birds, lizards, and insects, and they visually ground my garden in Central Texas, giving it a strong sense of place. I want my garden to look like home and *be* a home, in every sense.

What that looks like is this. Silver-green and powder-blue plants

OPPOSITE: Shaggy Berkeley sedge replaced St. Augustine lawn in the shady front yard. Yucca, salvia, and grasses provide deer-resistant texture and screening along the street.

FOLLOWING PAGE: A stock-tank planter accented with a blue-glass bottle bush is the focal point of the circle garden.

shimmer in the sunniest spaces: strappy, sawtoothed Wheeler's sotol; spherical beaked yucca with its grass-skirt trunk; whale's tongue agave shaped like a big blue rose; the pleated-fan leaves of dwarf palmetto; and creeping tendrils of woolly stemodia. Instead of traditional turfgrass, a patch of meadowy sedge makes a green negative space in the front garden, while requiring less water and only a single annual mowing in late spring. To screen the street and surrounding driveways, I planted taller and bushier plants around the perimeter and in the island bed of my circular drive. A gravel patio near the front door provides a spot for a couple of inviting chairs. In the side yard, a hanging swing chair and rustic bench add more places to sit and enjoy the garden.

In back, terraced beds and paths slow runoff during gullywasher rainstorms, helping to prevent erosion. A curvy swimming pool with circular patios at each end was installed by previous owners, and I riffed on all the roundness by making a circle garden where a small lawn used to be. An 8-foot-diameter, galvanized steel stock tank—formerly a goldfish pond, now a raised bed for agaves, wildflowers, and flowering bulbs, accented with a rebar-stemmed bottle bush—anchors the space. Encircling it, I laid chopped-stone paving in a sunburst design. Clipped globes of 'Winter Gem' boxwood make living gateposts for four paths leading into this crossroads-like space. When viewed from above—from a raised deck at the back door—the garden's circular geometry appears even more striking.

Inspired by visits to desert gardens that use colorful stucco walls as seating and architectural accents, I designed three walls of my own. Two charcoal gray walls that function as extra seating curve around the pool patios. A taller cobalt blue wall makes a color-block focal point behind the pool. Beaked yuccas stand like bobblehead sentinels in the background. Shade-tolerant perennials like 'Amistad' salvia, forsythia sage, beautyberry, white mistflower, chile pequin, Turk's cap, and firecracker fern fill the understory, supplemented by golden yuccas, grasses, and small trees like Texas mountain laurel, Mexican plum, Eve's necklace, Texas redbud, evergreen sumac, and pomegranate.

A garden is a process, not a finished project. It changes from season to season and year to year, often in ways that make my heart sing for the beauty of a happy plant combo, or a bonanza of blooms, or the privilege of watching wild creatures raise their young in the garden, like the screech owls that nested year after year in the owl box. Sometimes, though, favorite plants fall victim to weather or deer damage or who knows what. Most of it is beyond my control. Gardening teaches humility and patience above all else.

Weather extremes in recent years have caused me to reevaluate certain plants, especially semi-tender agaves (oh how I loved them) and formerly dependable evergreen shrubs like 'Soft Caress' mahonia and loropetalum. Increasingly, plants in Central Texas must be able to handle two or three months of 100°F highs while also enduring the occasional winter plunge to 10°F—or even 5°F, like during Winter Storm Uri in 2021. My plant palette may be contracting, but the garden as a whole is growing hardier and more resilient. The two hard-won yet simple gardening lessons still hold: plant what wants to live here, and just keep planting.

ABOVE: Annual 'Fireworks' gomphrena flowers exuberantly spring through fall.

LEFT: Pam Penick built her garden to meet the challenges of deer, dry shade, and a rocky, sloping lot.

ABOVE: Mexican beautyberry adds drama with clusters of dark purple berries in fall, earning its other name, black beautyberry.

RIGHT: Waterwise potted plants—foxtail fern, 'Frazzle Dazzle' dyckia, and succulents—harmonize with the yellow-green front door.

ABOVE: A steel planter overflows with Mexican feathergrass, globemallow, and purple heart against a blue stucco wall, as two 'Sapphire Skies' beaked yuccas peek over.

RIGHT: Pale pink 'Country Girl' chrysanthemum and dappled 'Moonglow' mangave make a pastel pairing.

ABOVE: Plants in the driveway's island bed screen the house from the street, including Turk's cap, bamboo muhly, Lindheimer's nolina, blue anise sage, silver Mediterranean fan palm, rosemary, and 'Vertigo' pennisetum.

LEFT: Pink 'Labuffarosa' rain lily and red oxblood lily pop up in the stock-tank planter with the first fall rain. Native woolly stemodia makes a silver-green carpet.

BELOW: 'Fiercely Fabulous' mangave sunbakes on a pedestal of stacked concrete pavers in two sizes. 'Dark Blue' plumbago, 'Little Grapes' gomphrena, and 'Pam Puryear' pink Turk's cap add soft flower color.

ABOVE LEFT: A metal prickly pear wreath adorns a steel-mesh gate.

LEFT: A squid agave in a culvert pipe planter is embraced by white mistflower.

ABOVE: Yellow-edged 'Opal' American agave perches above a dry-shade micro-meadow of Mexican feathergrass and society garlic. 'Baby Gem' boxwood balls are echoed by green gazing globes scattered in the grasses.

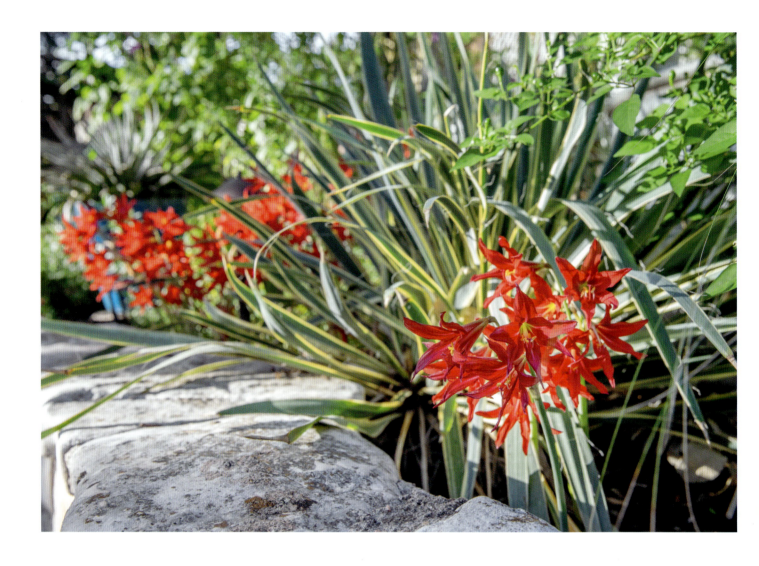

ABOVE: Oxblood lily blazes in early fall backed by 'Bright Edge' yucca.

OPPOSITE: 1/ **Sweet almond verbena** scents the garden with bottlebrush white flowers. 2/ **Ghost plant** spills from a Texas license-plate planter. 3/ A damselfly rests on **Texas sotol**. 4/ **Variegated whale's tongue agave, silver ponyfoot,** and **woolly stemodia** make a silvery combo. 5/ Metal animals mingle with potted agaves and a **mammillaria cactus**. 6/ An anole hunts insects on **Mexican flame vine**. 7/ **Golden thryallis** adds sunny color in the side garden. 8/ **'Opal' American agave** shows the ghostly imprints left behind by furled leaves. 9/ **Dwarf palmetto**'s arching stems of glaucous blue berries feed wildlife.

1

2

3

4

5

6

7

8

9

Repeat Materials, Colors, and Shapes for Harmony

To create harmony in your garden, repeat your design choices throughout. Pick a particular material, color, or shape, and use it over and over. The effect is pleasing to the eye, and since these are hardscaping elements (i.e., the manmade, non-plant portion of the garden), they'll look good all year, no matter what your plants are doing. Here's how I did that in my circle garden.

» **REPEAT MATERIALS** I started with a galvanized metal stock tank as the central focal point. I repeated the silver metal with three sections of culvert pipe that I turned into planters for squid agaves under the trees. Opposite, along the deck, three more silver planters contain small yuccas. More galvanized metal appears on the shed roof, a mirror on the fence, and a tall container under the mirror.

» **CHOOSE A COLOR PALETTE** To complement all that silver metal, I added a blue-glass bottle bush and other cobalt accents, including a blue stucco wall by the pool—a cooling color scheme in a hot Texas garden. Silvery plants like whale's tongue agave and woolly stemodia harmonize with the blues.

» **ECHO SHAPES** Circles, circles, and more circles orbit around the stock tank like planets around a sun. Chopped stone laid in a sunburst pattern around the tank emphasizes the circular geometry of the space, especially when seen from the elevated deck. The mirror, pipe planters, and 'Winter Gem' boxwood balls add more roundness. Also, linear indentations in the galvanized metal of the stock tank, pipe planters, and shed roof tie in with the radiating lines of the sunburst paving.

Deer-Resistant Plants for Dappled Shade

1/ **'Amistad' salvia** (*Salvia 'Amistad'*): rich-purple flowers spring through fall attract pollinators and hummingbirds. 2/ **Texas sotol** (*Dasylirion texanum*): evergreen toothy leaves catch sunlight, so plant it where morning or afternoon sun shines through it. 3/ **Mexican feathergrass** (*Nassella tenuissima*): graceful small grass with feathery, blond flowers in spring. 4/ **Bamboo muhly** (*Muhlenbergia dumosa*): billowing chartreuse foliage and upright, arching form reminiscent of bamboo. 5/ **Dwarf palmetto** (*Sabal minor*): evergreen fan-shaped leaves with excellent cold and heat tolerance. 6/ **Garlic chives** (*Allium tuberosum*): grassy foliage with bee-attracting white flower clusters in early fall. 7/ **Pale-leaf yucca** (*Yucca pallida*): blue-green, sword-shaped leaves with white flower spikes in spring. 8/ **Pale pavonia** (*Pavonia hastata*): pink-veined white flowers with a burgundy center and semi-evergreen foliage. May die in severe freezes but usually reseeds itself. 9/ **Golden thryallis** (*Galphimia glauca*): evergreen shrub in mild winters with upright stems of yellow flowers summer through fall.

WEST
TEXAS

THE PLACE

West Texas is a place of sky. A 180-degree sky that's a blue dome by day, and by night a pinpricked black expanse smeared by the Milky Way. Cauliflower-shaped thunderheads towering over grassland plains. Tangerine-and-violet sunsets. Ridges of volcanic mountains craggy on the horizon.

CLIMATE

Semiarid to arid. Summers are hot, but nights are usually cool. Winters are chilly, with gusty winds into spring. Snowfall is light except in the Panhandle, which averages nearly 18 inches of snow annually. Rainfall occurs primarily during the monsoon from June through September or October, averaging between 10 and 20 inches.

CHALLENGES AHEAD

Summers are growing hotter and longer, and monsoon rains are spottier and less predictable. Droughts are expected to become more severe, increasing the risk of wildfire.

TAKE ACTION

- ☐ Install gutters and cisterns to collect and store rainwater.

- ☐ Install drip irrigation, which is less wasteful and more targeted than overhead sprinklers. Drip is sometimes exempt from municipal watering restrictions because of its efficiency.

- ☐ Choose native plants, which evolved to survive the weather extremes of their native range, and well-adapted nonnatives that can tolerate record highs and lows, not just average temps.

- ☐ Create shade by planting desert-hardy trees on the southwest and southeast sides of the garden and by building pergolas or installing shade sails over patios.

- ☐ Plant a desert grassland garden instead of lawn, where appropriate. For areas of lawn, opt for low-water turf like buffalograss or Habiturf.

- ☐ Practice fire-wise landscaping if you live near grassland or canyon.

MODERN CAMP

"EVERYTHING ABOUT IT, I love," says Neil Subin of his remote home and garden atop a ridge in Casa Piedra, overlooking Big Bend country. "I love staring at San Jacinto, the mountain to the south. I love seeing the ribbon of cottonwoods along the creek. In the summertime when it rains, it's as green as Ireland. It's stunning." Neil dubbed his 1100-acre property MoFN Ranch—short for "Middle of F*cking Nowhere"—and relishes the isolation of the place, which he shares with deer, quail, roadrunners, foxes, coyotes, tarantulas, and the occasional rattlesnake. "There've been mountain lions on neighboring ranches' wildlife cams," he adds, though he has yet to spot one.

Before he came to West Texas, Neil had been an East Coaster with a love for ocean views. He grew up in New York and then built his business—he's CEO of a family office—and raised two kids in Florida. But fifteen years ago, concerned about climate change and its impact on the Florida coast, he began looking for acreage to build a second home protected from sea-level rise, with access to water, plenty of solitude, and proximity to culture, food, and art. Thirty minutes south of Marfa along Ranch Road 169—"one of the most beautiful roads I've driven," says Neil—he found his refuge. The land was part of the Dixon Water Foundation, and Neil struck a deal with them to preserve and never develop most of his property, along with a couple of thousand acres that the foundation retains. "You can't subdivide it," says Neil. "You can't do anything else to it.

Permanently. There's very little of this—large, undeveloped ranches—on the planet, and it deserves to be protected."

Across a caliche ridgetop, Neil designed and built several detached Galvalume metal structures: a bunkhouse, kitchen, primary bedroom, and guesthouse. "I thought about it in the context of a camp for adults," he says. "When I think about modern camps, that aesthetic is corrugated metal. It's very low maintenance. The conditions here are brutal, and it's resilient." A Corten steel pergola shelters a grilling area and outdoor table off the kitchen, but otherwise the landscape lies open to the sky. "The stars are insane," says Neil. To soften the hard lines of the metal structures and create some shade, he hired Alia Gunnell, owner of West Texas Roots, to landscape the site with plants tough enough to withstand the exposed, arid conditions. "I wanted a minimalist vibe," says Neil, "with as much native or native-like specimens as possible. I'm very attracted to agave and sotol. They're beautiful plants."

Alia looked for ways to tone down the glaring light and connect the buildings with garden beds. "It was all just white caliche," she recalls of the exposed, cement-like hardpan. "It was really bright, especially with those metal buildings. We needed

OPPOSITE: Whale's tongue agave thrives on the exposed ridgetop, where a firepit patio offers a gathering place under the big sky.

FOLLOWING PAGE: Bermed garden beds shelter a supersized steel firepit from buffeting wind.

natural, neutral colors to soften that. And there are multiple buildings and they're kind of spread out, so it was about trying to make it feel like one property by connecting the buildings." Alia built large raised beds encircled with rusty orange and gray boulders, elevating plants above the rock-hard caliche and defining sitting spaces and paths wide enough for Neil's ATV and maintenance vehicles. "The raised beds make you feel more protected," says Alia. The cottonwoods that Neil admires along Alamito Creek are too thirsty for the ridgetop, but Alia knew that feathery mesquite trees would thrive. She planted supremely heat- and drought-tolerant agave, yucca, ocotillo, and hesperaloe—architectural plants that Neil appreciates. She also urged him to include flowering native perennials and wildflowers like skeleton-leaf goldeneye, autumn sage, four-nerve daisy, yellow bells, Apache plume, and penstemon. Their looser, softer habit contrasts with the stiff, evergreen shapes of agave and yucca, and they erupt with colorful flowers when the monsoon rains come in summer, drawing in hummingbirds, bees, butterflies, wasps, and other pollinators. Neil was surprised by how much he enjoyed the color and winged activity that the flowering plants brought to the garden. "The wildflower component, that was Alia," says Neil. "I kind of resisted it. I like generally monochromatic things, with very small touches of color, and I didn't know it was going to work. But now I love it." Across the whole site, as a finishing touch, Alia spread a layer of tan gravel to cover the glaring white caliche.

A supersized Corten firepit surrounded by minimalist wooden chairs anchors the center of the garden. Raised beds surround the seating area, providing wind protection on chilly evenings. A barrel

sauna, square Corten plunge pool, and contemporary pergola that does triple duty as hammock hanger, movie-screen holder, and bocce court offer even more ways to enjoy the garden. Behind the bunkhouse, another firepit provides a secondary gathering place. It overlooks a stone patio with planting pockets for a dozen Texas sotols, and beyond that, a horizon of rounded hills. While Neil appreciates the solitude of the ranch—"you're 30 miles from town, 5 miles from your nearest neighbor, and staring 60 miles into nothing in the landscape," he says—he also likes to host family and friends for unplugged time around the fire, lounging in hammocks, grilling, and watching movies under the stars. The atomized design of his home encourages being outdoors. Walking through the garden multiple times each day and evening is part of the experience.

Five wells on the property provide water for Neil's home and garden, although the garden isn't connected to an irrigation system. Alia has been hand-watering the new garden to get it established, but she points out that the waterwise native plants are already largely able to fend for themselves. "This spot gets so hot," she says, "and it rains even less here than in Marfa. But for two weeks we were all out of town, and we didn't have to worry about it. It all looked great. That's always my goal."

For Neil, the experience of living in this dramatic and wide-open landscape has been transformed by his garden of native plants. "The flowers and the wildlife they attract, the butterflies, the hummingbirds—getting up in the morning and seeing that is inspiring," he says. "The garden is beautiful on its own. But between the color and the wildlife, the dynamic it creates is extraordinary. I didn't expect it."

ABOVE: Behind a grouping of beaked yucca, Havard agave, and Texas sage, a breezeway frames a view of distant hills.

LEFT: Designer Alia Gunnell, pictured with her dogs Kiva (front) and Turk, maintains the new garden and waters by hand as needed.

ABOVE: Silver-leaved Texas sage erupts with violet flowers when it rains or in anticipation of rain, responding to changes in humidity, earning it the common name of barometer plant.

RIGHT: Yellow flowers of desert marigold bring sunshine to earth.

OPPOSITE: A feathery-leaved honey mesquite tree is xeric enough to grow on the arid ridge and will provide light shade as it matures.

OPPOSITE, TOP: A long-tongued sphinx moth sips nectar from an autumn sage blossom.

OPPOSITE, BOTTOM: A second firepit behind the bunkhouse is bordered by a grid of Texas sotols tucked into planting pockets in the flagstone paving.

ABOVE: Broad paths through the bermed planting beds allow for ATV and truck access when needed.

ABOVE: Along the gravel drive, Faxon yucca, Texas sage, Gregg's mistflower, and other native plants make a pocket garden of color and texture.

OPPOSITE, CLOCKWISE FROM TOP: A minimalist steel arbor supports a row of hammocks and a screen for watching movies under the stars.

Agarita's holly-like leaves offer evergreen texture. Honey-scented yellow flowers appear in spring, followed by red berries that feed birds and small mammals.

The MoFN Ranch gate spotlights the property's remote location.

Foil Bad Soil

If you have concrete-hard caliche or rocky soil, get on top of it. That is, build raised beds or berms that you can easily plant in. You won't have to get out the breaker bar, plants will grow better and faster, and the height adds dimension to a flat lot. To figure out where to put a raised bed and how large to make it, think through how you can leverage its height—and the added height of plants growing in it—for wind protection, privacy screening, and hiding unwelcome views. Also consider how it will impact drainage patterns.

In Neil's garden, Alia built large planting berms right on top of the caliche, mounding trucked-in soil about 4 feet high in the center. Large boulders hold the soil in place. She watered the berms well for a couple of weeks to allow for settling before planting. Expect raised beds to continue settling over the first year, and plan accordingly when making them.

Plants for Rocky, Dry Conditions

1/ **Beaked yucca** (*Yucca rostrata*): strappy, blue-green leaves are held like a sunburst atop a grassy trunk. 2/ **Whale's tongue agave** (*Agave ovatifolia*): solitary (non-pupping) agave with powder blue, cupped, toothy leaves tipped with mahogany spines. 3/ **Autumn sage** (*Salvia greggii*): small shrub with minty leaves and hummingbird-attracting pink, red, violet, or salmon flowers. 4/ **Yellow bells** (*Tecoma stans*): bell-shaped yellow flowers from spring to fall attract bees and hummingbirds. 5/ **Ocotillo** (*Fouquieria splendens*): spiny, upright stems are typically bare but leaf out after a rain, when crimson flower clusters appear at the tips. 6/ **Apache plume** (*Fallugia paradoxa*): branching shrub with white, rose-like flowers followed by light-catching, feathery pink seedheads.

GROUNDED IN GRASSLAND

"**EVERYBODY IS FAMILIAR** with cacti and agaves and ocotillos," says Jim Martinez, a landscape designer and soil scientist who lives on the edge of town in Marfa with partner Jim Fissel. "Those are beautiful, but the reality is there are 3000 different species in the Chihuahuan Desert. My intent was to do a garden where people could see all the things that grow in this desert. I wanted it to be about the place that it's in."

That place is the Trans-Pecos, a vast arid landscape in the westernmost part of Texas. It's home to at least 268 grass species and 447 species of woody plants, a surprising diversity considering the illusion of a lot of nothing—just tawny grass under a big sky and volcanic mountains on the horizon—when cruising through at highway speed. When you slow down and look, though, you see much more. "If you walk in the grassland," says Jim, "you realize these are all bunchgrasses, and they have spacing between them because that's how they absorb moisture. And within the grasses there are all these forbs that bloom." Wildlife thrives in grassland, including birds, deer, antelope, rabbits, javelina, insects, and reptiles. However, much of the Trans-Pecos grassland is used for cattle ranching, says Jim, and "cattle graze everything down every year. There's nothing left for the other things that evolved here, the birds, the insects. So my feeling is, if you use water wisely and recreate these environments in your garden, even if it's just a postage-stamp-sized garden, every bird in the area is going to come there. Bees, butterflies, lizards, insects, you name it, because you're the only little niche that has what they need."

Jim and his partner purchased their 1¼-acre lot in 1999, while they were living in Dallas but coming out to Marfa to hike and explore. Two national parks, Big Bend and Guadalupe Mountains, are within an hour to two hours' drive. "Texas is a big place," says Jim wryly. "If you have to drive a hundred miles, that's nothing. That's like going to the grocery store." Even before they built their house and relocated to Marfa, Jim started planting the garden. Every five weeks or so, he'd drive out from Dallas to work in the garden, tucking new plants along a sheltering windbreak of Arizona cypress. He'd water them in and leave, and weeks later he'd return to see what survived long enough to receive another deep soaking. This experimentation showed him which plants could make it largely on their own in a region that receives a scant 15 inches of rain a year, with most of that falling during the summer monsoon from June through September. The remainder of the year, rain is a memory.

When the disruption of home construction was over, Jim began sowing desert grasses to make a central meadow. Overlooked by the back porch and two small guesthouses, the meadow awakens each morning to the clear notes of birdsong, its feathery or tufted grass stems incandescing as the golden light catches them. "It took about five years to get it to what it is today," says Jim. "I took seed from other areas and spread it there, and I bought seed from native grass suppliers."

Flowing around a thicket of elbowbush— a small native tree with berries and cover for

OPPOSITE: Stone pine and yucca spring from a swath of silver-tipped cane bluestem.

FOLLOWING PAGE: The meadow garden catches the morning light.

birds and nectar-rich flowers for insects—grasses ripple in the breeze and ripen in color through the seasons. Bull muhly, deer muhly, curly mesquite, sacaton, and bluestem are some of Jim's favorites. Grama grasses have special significance. Jim, who has American Indian ancestry, says that blue grama figures into a creation story for indigenous people. "When the first woman was put on Earth," he relates, "she was lonely and asked the creator if she could have a child. She's given a child, but the monsters that roam the world take the child and eat it. This happens again and again. But she's able to hide one child until he's older, and he asks for guidance on how to survive the monsters. He is shown how to make a bow from a willow and an arrow from grama grass to shoot the monsters and kill them. And that's what he does. The context is, the monster is starvation, right? If you keep the grassland intact, there's always wildlife that will keep you alive."

Jim grew up in New Mexico, tasked with taking care of his family's yard and garden. "My parents gave me carte blanche," he says, "and we had a lot of gardening friends, and they gave me plants. I was always outside." His grandmother sparked his interest in native plants. "She had this magical green thumb, but she was also an herbalist," he recalls. "When I would visit her during the summer—I was twelve or thirteen years old—we would go collect herbs in the mountains. We'd spend four days and end up each evening at a relative's house to spend the night. She showed me how to collect and not give out the source because people come and take everything. You take just a little bit and never let anyone know where they are."

In his twenties, Jim traveled to Europe to see gardens, which he describes as a turning point in his thinking about garden design and plants. "I got to London, Paris, Spain, Italy," he says, "and I knew all the plants. There was nothing new. They were all using the same Chinese, Indian, New Zealand, and Australian plants. I was there for the discovery of their native plants, but they were not using them. I enjoyed and learned a lot from their designs. But as far as plants, I was disappointed." Back home, Jim segued from fieldwork in soil science to managing a landscaping company. By the early 1990s, he had his own design firm in Dallas and was designing gardens with whatever natives were available. "Salvias were being introduced and a few other things," he says. "I was including native grasses, perennials, and shrubs into the traditional landscape design of city gardens, which sometimes are plant deserts for birds. There's nothing there for them to eat. I was trying to steer my clients away from that."

Over the past twenty years in West Texas, Jim has established himself as an expert on native plants of the Chihuahuan Desert, and on grassland species in particular. His partner, Jim Fissel, also takes a keen interest in plants and gardening. Together they co-authored the book *Marfa Garden*—along with writer Martha Hughes and photographer Mary Lou Saxon—which showcases desert grassland species that they're growing in their garden. They hope it will encourage other West Texans to grow more of these remarkable plants, not only for their beauty and wildlife habitat, but because they're part of a vitally important ecosystem. "Grasslands around the world, they're only maybe 30 percent of the landmass," says Jim, "but they sequester more carbon than all the forests in the world."

Grassland gardens are about change and discovery, adds Jim. The couple enjoys walking the paths through their garden, admiring new growth and identifying birdsong with the Merlin app on their phones. "It's calming," he says. "We sit and watch the meadow and the birds. It's not really exciting, but it's pretty wonderful."

ABOVE: Purple flower buds of tansyleaf tansyaster prepare to unfurl in response to monsoon rains.

LEFT: Jim Fissel and Jim Martinez enjoy watching for painted buntings and other seed-eating birds drawn to the grasses.

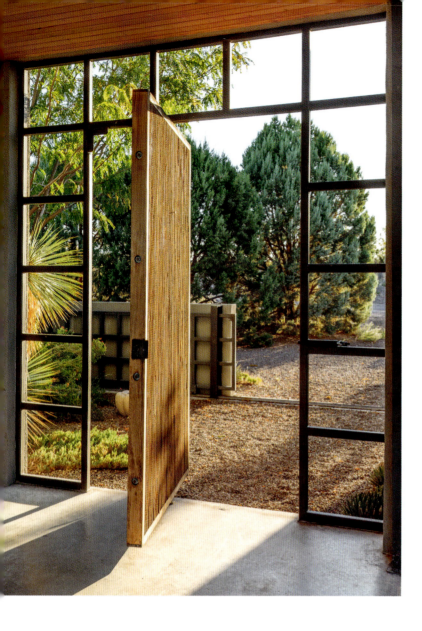

ABOVE: A pivoting door between the porch and front garden admits breezes and views.

RIGHT: Eastern Mojave buckwheat, a bee favorite, shows off popcorn-like clusters of pinkish white flowers.

ABOVE: Beaked yucca and pinyon pine add bristly foliage amid cane bluestem.

RIGHT: Canyon senna is a showy shrub with bright yellow flowers and long, flat seedpods.

ABOVE LEFT: A house finch arrives for an evening drink from the birdbath.

LEFT: Columbine seedheads remain attractive long after flowers have faded.

ABOVE: Two guesthouses look out on the meadow garden and stone pines.

OPPOSITE, TOP: Groovestem bouchea's purple flowers and narrow, green stems stand out against a painted stucco wall.

OPPOSITE, BOTTOM: The contemporary home's L-shaped porch overlooks the meadow garden and offers good bird-watching opportunities.

ABOVE: A ground-level water bowl tucked amid the grasses attracts birds and other small creatures.

RIGHT: Cane bluestem's silver flowers glow when backlit.

How to Maintain a Desert Garden

» **WATER LESS IN WINTER** All plants have specific needs, and desert plants are no exception. When a native desert garden fails to thrive, says Jim, it's often the result of watering at the wrong time of year. "You have to remember that these plants evolved with ¾ of the year being dry," he says, "so you can't water them the same amount year-round."

The dry season in West Texas starts in October and lasts until June or July, when the monsoon arrives. During the cool part of the dry season, a native plant garden needs much less water—maybe once or twice a month at most, says Jim. In gardens with automatic irrigation, if the sprinklers run as often in the cool season as they do in the hot summer, plants may rot. Switch the irrigation system to manual in the cool season, and turn it on sparingly.

» **LET GRASSES STAND THROUGH WINTER** Desert grassland gardens offer beauty and wildlife habitat throughout the year, but not if they're chopped back too early. Leave grasses standing until late winter or early spring, advises Jim. "Birds need that grassy environment in winter," he says. "They eat whatever seed is left, and they need it for cover." Also, grasses have beautiful winter color and movement in the wind. "If you cut them back too early, you're depriving yourself of their beauty," says Jim. Cut grasses back in early May, and they'll start to regrow right away.

» **KEEP YOUR CUTTINGS** Instead of bagging and throwing away cut-back grasses, Jim strews them across his garden. "We don't throw anything away," he says. "We use every bit of that material. We either compost the clippings or scatter them to make sure the garden has organic matter." As grasses reshoot, they quickly hide the cuttings. "And because Texas is so hot," says Jim, "the cuttings decompose very quickly," feeding the soil in the process. Make sure any weeds, however, go in the compost to avoid spreading their seeds in the garden.

Grasses for West Texas

1/ **Blue grama** (*Bouteloua gracilis*): short, tufty grass with blond seedheads held horizontally like pennants. 2/ **Sideoats grama** (*Bouteloua curtipendula*): oat-like seeds are held along one side of the stems like fringe on a suede jacket. 3/ **Mexican feathergrass** (*Nassella tenuissima*): low, upright grass with bright green foliage in spring that turns tan in summer, and fluffy, blond flowers that undulate in a breeze. 4/ **Alkali sacaton** (*Sporobolus airoides*): upright, gray-green grass with a graceful scrim of feathery, reddish seedheads. 5/ **Cane bluestem** (*Bothriochloa barbinodis*): tufts of silvery white seedheads held above foliage that blushes reddish yellow. 6/ **Green sprangletop** (*Leptochloa dubia*): thin, branching seedheads held aloft over blue-green wiry stems.

INVITING NATURE IN

"**THE GENESIS OF** the garden was humiliation," cracks Guy Fielder. When he and wife Lisa bought their 1909 bungalow in Alpine, they were pleased with its large corner lot—almost an acre—but not its condition. "There was nothing here but goatheads, a few tumbleweeds, and one dead tree," recalls Lisa. "We knew we were going to have to do something. It was just incredibly hideous."

The Fielders had lived all over Texas—in Houston and Austin in their working years and as they raised two sons, and in Midland in retirement—and they'd never given much thought to gardening beyond maintaining lawn, groundcovers, and trees. That changed when they settled in Alpine in 2021 with the intention of opening a commercial brewery and beer garden with their son Tim, a brewer. Faced with the goathead burr–infested blank slate of a yard, they hired local designer and native plant conservationist Michael Eason to design a low-water garden of native plants with no lawn. "We did not dream he could put together something like this," says Lisa. "So many people, including us, who have lived in Texas all their lives don't realize how many beautiful native plants there are here. They just have no idea what's possible. We certainly didn't. We're just amazed."

Today, blazing red salvias and tawny-plumed grasses muscle up to each other in undulating raised beds on each side of the front walk. Rocket-shaped yellow columbine lights up the garden by the hundreds in spring, and lemon-yellow puffballs of sweet acacia—"they look like miniature fireworks," says Lisa—waft their honeyed fragrance. Responding to the monsoon rains, aromatic slenderleaf sage turns into a bumblebee magnet with masses of indigo flowers, and datura's white, salad plate–sized blossoms unfurl at dusk to draw in sphinx moths. Native morning glory vine displays lilac, tissue-petaled flowers as it twines up the trunk of a young bur oak, one of several oaks planted for shade and wildlife habitat. Along the public sidewalk, feathery sand sage and Apache plume make a touchable, silver-and-pink border. Meandering around the island beds, wide gravel paths invite exploring and sitting at one of the tables placed throughout the garden.

The wildlife that the garden attracts—birds, insects of all kinds, lizards—astonishes and delights the Fielders, who are both certified as Texas master naturalists. "We have so many different types of bees and wasps of all sizes," marvels Lisa, "from tiny things about ⅜ of an inch long to giant tarantula hawks. We're discovering wonderful butterflies and caterpillars that we've never seen before. Hummingbirds visit some of the flowers. We also have lizards and geckos. We're amazed how much nature has shown up." Accompanied by ChaCha, the couple's Havanese pup, Guy putters in the garden for a couple of hours most mornings, pulling weeds, trimming plants, or watering to get the young garden established. All the while he keeps an eager eye out for pollinators and other creatures drawn to the oasis. "One morning it was air-traffic central," he says. "There were hundreds of dragonflies, grasshoppers, butterflies, moths. Six or seven varieties of bees. Hummingbirds. All just buzzing around. The air was filled with them."

OPPOSITE: Darcy's sage echoes the red door and metal roof of the hundred-year-old house.

FOLLOWING PAGE: Four-nerve daisy and damianita add sunny color to a rocky bed with whale's tongue agave and a tarantula sculpture by local artist Harry Weekley.

In their walled side garden, an octagonal metal gazebo newly planted with hop vines shelters an outdoor dining table. The couple enjoys entertaining here, cooking on the grill and watching the stars in the famously dark West Texas sky. "Part of the reason we came to Alpine is because you can live outdoors for much of the year," says Guy. After Lisa attended a five-week cooking school on an organic farm in Ireland, she was inspired to install raised beds for growing their own food. "We'd never grown a vegetable or herb in our lives," she says. "We're still learning when to plant and how to space them, but we've enjoyed produce from our garden all summer long. We're growing things that we cannot buy locally, like lovage, chives, and eggplants."

Lisa and Guy take pleasure in sharing their garden with others and have invited local chapters of the Texas Master Gardener Program, Texas Master Naturalist Program, and Native Plant Society of Texas to visit. Drop-in visitors are welcome too, says Lisa. "We would love to see neighbors stroll by and have a seat in the garden or look at the plant labels and see what the plants are," she says. "We would love this to be almost a park-like place for this little part of Alpine." They hope the beauty of the plants and the wildlife they attract will inspire others to convert their yards to native plant gardens. "We're concerned that insect populations and bird populations are in decline," says Guy. "So we wanted a garden that would foster insects, which would then support the birds. We don't spray or poison anything."

Michael, the garden's designer, agrees it's important to grow native plants to create more stopovers and habitat for wildlife. "The more we learn," he says, "about how native plants have co-evolved with all the various pollinators and insects and how much damage we are doing and how much we are losing daily, we should be trying to provide as much habitat as possible for these animals. These are small gardens in some cases, but over time they do make a difference."

When Michael talks about native plants, he means plants that are locally native and sourced from a grower close to home, not native plants from other parts of the state or the country. He admits it can take more effort to locate locally grown native plants, but he says there's a network of smaller growers throughout the state to tap into.

Watering and the infrastructure of their hundred-year-old home were a concern for Guy and Lisa from the start. Before installing the garden, the couple replaced the decrepit water and sewer pipes that ran through the yard to the house. "I'm a belt-and-suspenders person," explains Guy. "Before we put in all these expensive flowerbeds, we replaced the lines. They're under the flowerbeds now, but hopefully it'll last beyond our lifetimes. If we'd left the old lines, they could have failed at any time." The couple also repaired an old well on their property and connected the garden's drip-irrigation system to it—"so we're not using city water," says Lisa—and they're installing several large cisterns to collect rainwater off their roof. "The first few years, we have to water to make sure the plants stay healthy while they're building their root systems," says Lisa. "But we think after that, we will only have to water in drought situations."

The garden has been a learning process every step of the way, but Lisa and Guy have been surprised by how much joy it brings them. "The garden requires a little more maintenance than what we expected," admits Lisa, "but we're not disappointed by that. We don't see it as a chore. We actually enjoy it." From a cost perspective, the couple believes their xeriscape garden will pay off in the long run because they won't ever have to mow and will seldom need to water to keep their plants looking good. It's already paying dividends in daily wonder. "Let nature happen," urges Lisa. "Caterpillars will eat your plants. Strange insects will show up. But it's wonderful, so embrace it and encourage it. Enjoy letting nature in. It's been such a delight for us."

ABOVE: Feathery pink seed-heads of Apache plume glow in the sunlight.

LEFT: Guy and Lisa Fielder, pictured with their dog, ChaCha, enjoy seeing all the wildlife drawn to their garden oasis.

ABOVE: Brushland shrubverbena makes a mound of delicate, purple-and-white flowers.

RIGHT: A hummingbird watches over the garden from its ocotillo perch.

OPPOSITE: Cliff morning glory twines into an oak tree.

OPPOSITE, TOP: Climbing hop vines will soon cloak an octagonal gazebo built over an existing brick patio.

OPPOSITE, BOTTOM: Lisa and Guy enjoy dining under the gazebo. Down-facing lights lessen light pollution at night, helping to keep the Big Bend area a prime spot for stargazing.

ABOVE: Multiple patio tables offer visitors plenty of spots to sit and enjoy the front garden.

ABOVE: Lindheimer's muhly and Darcy's sage, planted in bermed beds, screen the inner garden from the street.

OPPOSITE, CLOCKWISE FROM TOP LEFT:
A bumblebee straddles a yellow bells flower.

Red glass flowers sparkle on a barbed-wire-and-rebar ocotillo by Harry Weekley.

The indigo blossoms of slenderleaf sage attract bees by the dozens.

Darcy's sage blazes against a gray-green wall.

Use Native Plants for Any Garden Style

Interest in growing natives has skyrocketed in Texas since the 1980s, the early years of the native plant movement. Even so, many people assume natives are only suitable for naturalistic gardens or wildscapes. If you (or your HOA) favor a more traditional, formal, or contemporary style, native plants can work equally as well as commonly available exotic plants like liriope, abelia, butterfly bush, and boxwood.

In designing Lisa and Guy's native plant garden, Michael envisioned a formal layout to complement the bungalow's symmetry. "The limestone path divides the front garden in two," he says. "We did a mirror image on either side of it with the exact same plants, everything symmetrical. The idea was a formal entrance as you're walking into this Chihuahuan Desert garden." On each side of the path, upright ocotillo takes the place of a nonnative small tree like crape myrtle. Instead of an exotic shrub like juniper, whale's tongue agave adds evergreen structure. And in place of plumbago or roses, yellow-flowering damianita and four-nerve daisy add perennial color. Woolly stemodia, a silvery groundcover, fills in around the river rock.

Native Pollinator Plants for West Texas

1/ **Yellow bells** (*Tecoma stans*): upright deciduous shrub with yellow, bell-shaped flowers from spring through fall. 2/ **Cliff morning glory** (*Ipomoea rupicola*): tissue-textured lavender flowers with violet centers adorn this diminutive twining vine. 3/ **Datura** (*Datura wrightii*): palm-sized, fragrant white flowers unfurl at twilight, attracting sphinx moths. 4/ **Devil's claw** (*Proboscidea parviflora*): sprawling annual with dark rose flowers and curved and hooked seedpods, which inspire its common name. 5/ **Darcy's sage** (*Salvia darcyi*): upright bushy perennial with abundant red flowers that attract hummingbirds.

6/ **Slenderleaf sage** (*Salvia reptans*): cobalt blue flowers cover sprawling, slender stems, enticing bees and hummingbirds. 7/ **Desert four o'clock** (*Mirabilis multiflora*): violet-pink flowers open in late afternoon—hence the common name—and close in the morning. 8/ **Four-nerve daisy** (*Tetraneuris scaposa*): petite tufts of green leaves, with yellow daisies on slender stems that bloom nearly year-round. 9/ **Apache plume** (*Fallugia paradoxa*): white flowers in spring and summer are followed by fluffy pink seedheads.

DESERT OASIS

A LOW GRAY-GREEN WALL sets off Susan Kirr and Rusty Martin's home from a busy residential intersection in Marfa. Between the wall and the road, purple prickly pear, starburst-headed yucca, and diminutive yellow wildflowers bravely thread a path. Protected within the wall, a sparely planted garden of powder-blue agave, fuzzy-spined prickly pear, and tangerine-flowered barrel cactus complements the modern-minimalist style of the renovated hundred-year-old adobe bungalow. But hidden from view of passersby, behind a head-high wall, is a desert oasis revealed when a gate of Corten steel pivots open. Inside, flame-flowered salvia, lavender puffs of mistflower, filamented passionflower, and fuchsia trumpets of desert willow hum and flutter with pollen-collecting bees, long-tongued sphinx moths, and stained-glass butterflies. Grasses catch sunlight in fizzy or feathery flower spikes, swaying with each breath of wind. Nothing could be more surprising after the restrained desert landscaping out front.

"We are in the desert, but I wanted it to be as lush as possible," says Susan. "Now, it's not lush like you would find in the Northeast. But for the desert, it's a little oasis. We wanted a lot of color and texture and flowers, hence some of the flowers that are not native, but they're mixed in so we can have big blooms for cutting and putting in the kitchen. We're just walking the line between the native environment and making it colorful and beautiful." Susan, a movie producer, and Rusty, a filmmaker and artist, relocated to Marfa after 21 years in Austin. Rusty tended their former garden. Susan takes the lead now. "I enjoy tending the garden," she says. "It's good exercise, I'm out in the sunshine, and I'm just quietly working away and beautifying the garden and keeping it healthy. Rusty and I also like to go out at dusk with our dog and just wander around. It's so hot here in the summertime, but in the early evening it's beautiful and quiet."

The half-acre garden is part of the property's transformation since Susan and Rusty purchased the house on the edge of town. Upstairs windows look out on grassland and mountains—the view was part of the appeal—but the house had sat vacant for twenty years. "It was a shell," says Susan. "It took us about two years to renovate it with the help of our builder, Billy Marginot. The back was literally a patch of dirt. There were some dead trees and one enormous yucca. It was such a wreck that we had to start from scratch." On the recommendation of their architect, Kristin Bonkemeyer, the couple hired local designer Jim Martinez in 2018 to reimagine their yard using mostly plants native to the Chihuahuan Desert, supplemented with annuals like zinnia for cutting and a few old favorites, like roses, from their Austin garden. "Jim is so talented design-wise and creatively," says Susan, "but he also really knows this area

OPPOSITE: Datura makes a fragrant, night-blooming mound in front of the garden gate. The flowers attract sphinx moths and bees until they close in the morning.

FOLLOWING PAGE: Raised beds overflow with asparagus and squash, and the pollinator garden blooms with abandon under monsoon clouds. In back, a peak-roofed shed draws the eye.

and knows native plants. Some plants he said, 'Don't even try that. It won't do well here.' I accepted his wisdom, and he guided us to things that *would* do well here."

The weeds had to be eradicated first, and Jim brought in lots of good soil for planting. Poured-concrete pads make a long, rhythmic path through the garden, ending at an expansive dining patio sheltered by a steel arbor. A deep perennial bed follows the path and separates the garden into two halves, with a vegetable garden and koi pond on one side and herbs, beehives, a smaller pond, and a buffalograss lawn on the other. "Between the gardens," says Jim, "there are pathways to cross and islands of mostly desert plants. Susan asked me to include some plants because she has a personal attachment to them. For me, that's what makes a garden a garden."

Susan particularly enjoys growing vegetables in the raised beds. "I plant in the spring and in the fall," she says, "and the secret is that the winter garden

is such a great opportunity. It's way better than the summer garden because things get kind of scorched here, and in July and August they just shut down. When you plant in September, it grows through May—beets and carrots and turnips and other good stuff. It's not easy to get organic food out here in the Big Bend, and I really love cooking it and canning it and baking with it." Watering three times a week on drip keeps the entire garden lush and full. Susan and Rusty have an irrigation system that draws on well water, plus a rainwater-collection cistern that holds 4000 gallons. "It's the best water for the plants," says Susan. "One rainstorm fills it up," adds Jim. In summer, the monsoon rains bring the garden into full flower. "The whole garden just opens up when the rains come," says Susan. "Some things only bloom when it rains, like Texas sage. They don't bloom when they're irrigated. They need a big drink from the sky, and then they're covered in purple blossoms."

Outside the walls, the garden isn't irrigated, so Susan planted the toughest desert plants she could find. "We have some land in Casa Piedra, about an hour south of Marfa," she says. "There's a prickly pear cactus there called 'Santa Rita', and it turns purple if it doesn't get too much water. I took a bunch of pads and stuck them in the ground, and they've done really well. They get these masses of blossoms almost like roses. From May to June, they're just glorious. And I harvest wildflower seeds from all around and throw them in there, and those are finally coming up."

Relying largely on native plants makes sense when gardening in the desert, says Susan. "We're being respectful of what the land can manage. It's not going to look like a New Jersey garden. It's going to look like a desert garden that you've taken a little time with. You have to be humble about what's possible out here and do the best you can with what you have, and not try to bend it to your will."

ABOVE: Darcy's sage and Russian sage glow in morning light.

LEFT: Rusty Martin and Susan Kirr enjoy the tranquility of their walled garden, where they keep bees and grow pollinator plants, vegetables, and favorite flowers for cutting.

OPPOSITE: A glass mosaic cow skull adds western style on an arbor post.

ABOVE: A monarch butterfly nectars on a zinnia flower.

RIGHT: 'Lynn's Legacy' Texas sage covers itself in lavender flowers in response to rain.

OPPOSITE: Pink cotton-candy flowers of Gulf muhly catch the morning light. Behind it, three kinds of salvia—Darcy's sage, Russian sage, and germander sage—attract pollinators.

OPPOSITE, TOP: Havard agave and bunny ears cactus add desert beauty to the sparely planted front courtyard.

OPPOSITE, BOTTOM: At the rear of the garden, a high steel arbor shelters a dining patio.

ABOVE: Wildflowers, cacti, and yuccas soften a low courtyard wall in front of the house.

ABOVE: Mountain sage, bull muhly grass, and datura flower under a desert willow.

OPPOSITE, CLOCKWISE FROM TOP LEFT: A tarantula hawk is another pollinator in the garden. Despite a fearsome sting designed for hunting tarantulas to feed its larvae, this large wasp is nonaggressive toward people.

A gently bubbling fountain provides a water source for thirsty bees and other pollinators.

A tufty buffalograss lawn needs little mowing or water. Corrugated metal sheaths a poly rainwater cistern for a more contemporary look.

Plant a Native Lawn

For a lawn without all the watering and mowing, consider buffalograss. A native turfgrass of the Great Plains, buffalograss is heat and cold tolerant and can survive on as little as 12 inches of rain a year. While it does not tolerate heavy foot traffic, it's well suited to all areas of the state except for wetter East Texas and along the coast. Narrow, blue-green blades grow slowly to about 5 or 8 inches. Left long, it ripples in the breeze like the prairie grass it is.

A buffalograss lawn requires unlearning traditional turf maintenance. It doesn't need fertilizing or regular mowing or watering. During drought (or during a dry summer), it goes dormant and turns tan, but it greens up again when it rains. Overwatering to keep it green makes it vulnerable to weed incursion, particularly Bermudagrass. It requires full sun, patience to establish by seed, regular weeding as it fills in, and thereafter a very light hand with watering and mowing.

The payoff is a fine-textured, meadowy native lawn that allows you to put away the mower, edger, fertilizers, and sprinklers and just enjoy its beauty.

Flower Power for Far West Texas

1/ 'Bubba' desert willow (*Chilopsis linearis* 'Bubba'): frilly, burgundy-and-pink blossoms put on a glorious summer show and attract bees, butterflies, and hummingbirds. **2/ 'Lynn's Legacy' Texas sage** (*Leucophyllum frutescens* 'Lynn's Legacy'): evergreen foliage erupts with violet flowers when humidity rises before and after it rains. **3/ Passionflower** (*Passiflora incarnata*): perennial vine with fantastical purple flowers and foliage that feeds caterpillars of several species of butterflies. **4/ Four-nerve daisy** (*Tetraneuris scaposa*): yellow daisies float above mounds of thready, green leaves. **5/ Mountain sage** (*Salvia regla*): shrubby perennial with showy red flowers beloved by hummingbirds. **6/ Darcy's sage** (*Salvia darcyi*): upright bushy perennial with abundant red flowers that attract hummingbirds. **7/ Zinnia** (*Zinnia elegans*): annual flower, easily grown by seed, that attracts bees, butterflies, and hummingbirds. **8/ Fishhook barrel cactus** (*Ferocactus wislizeni*): showy orange, yellow, or red flowers and pineapple-shaped fruits atop a ribbed, columnar barrel with fishhook spines. **9/ 'Rosalie Figge' bearded iris** (*Iris* 'Rosalie Figge'): satiny, dark purple flowers and sword-shaped leaves.

FAMILY RETREAT

ACROSS THE ROAD from Nancy Haywood's place, the barracks of historic Fort Davis back up to an imposing palisade of stone created 35 million years ago, when a volcano blasted open the earth and resculpted it with lava. That scenic ridge has been a playground for the Haywood family—Nancy and her late husband, Ted, and their three children and their families—for 23 years, ever since they started coming to the town of Fort Davis as a getaway from their primary residence in Houston. "Everyone loves to hike," says Nancy, "and the fort is just across the street, and you can go up all the trails and get to the top of the mountain."

Nancy and Ted purchased their distinctive adobe-and-stone house—"built in 1936, the year I was born," says Nancy affectionately—and in 2015 embarked on an extensive remodel, inside and out, to make it more livable. Set back from the road on a ¾-acre lot, the house looked out on lawn and trees then, mostly pecans, junipers, Arizona cypress, and a cottonwood in front and a couple of pears in back, survivors from an old home orchard. Along the drive, a red windmill and stone water tank added western charm, although the windmill no longer worked to pump water into the tank. It was all ripe for a redesign. "We were looking for a native garden," says Nancy. "I love native flowers and knew how difficult it would be if we had plants that weren't native to that area. And we wanted to be able to look out at a beautiful view from every window. We wanted the garden to be inside the house as well as outside." The couple brought in

Alpine-based designer Michael Eason to reimagine the front as a meadow garden with native wildflowers, grasses, cacti, and agaves. In back, they requested a cutting garden for Nancy and a bermed lawn for the grandchildren to play on. Michael started working on the garden even as construction on the house was ongoing, completing one section before moving to another. "The idea was a high diversity of plants," says Michael, "with a wildflower view in front, and then along the right side as you drive in, little pockets and vignettes."

Today a gravel path winds through colorful wild-flowers in spring and light-catching grasses in summer and fall, accented with evergreen agave, yucca, and prickly pear. Large boulders make impromptu spots to sit and enjoy the garden. "The rock outcroppings are like what you'd see in a grassy meadow in the Davis Mountains," explains Michael. In the side yard, the water tank beside the windmill was converted into a plunge pool, with steps and a stone terrace built around it. "It's a big draw," says Nancy. "One time the grandchildren were so hot from hiking across the street that they all jumped into it with their clothes on." At night, they sit on the pool terrace, she says, and explore the star-spangled sky through a telescope.

In back, a firepit with benches entices the family out to roast marshmallows for

OPPOSITE: Mexican grass tree's long, narrow leaves grow in a strappy sphere resembling a fiber-optic lamp.

FOLLOWING PAGE: A blue-gray whale's tongue agave accents a gravel patio with a steel-ring firepit.

s'mores. And as Nancy expected, the bermed lawn has proved popular with her five grandchildren. "We love to make up games where you have to run up the hill and throw the football five times and catch it or something," she says. "I'm the cheerleader. We give awards at the end and make ribbons. It's lots of fun for them." As for Nancy, she enjoys cutting flowers from her raised beds to make bouquets for the house and just soaking up the views from her sunporch. "We do a lot of reading out there and playing games," she says. "I love watching the hummingbirds, the bees, the butterflies feeding on the flowers."

Ted enjoyed the garden for several years before he passed away in 2020. Nancy and her family returned to Fort Davis to scatter Ted's ashes in the place he loved best. "We call it Ted's Garden now because we scattered some of his ashes in it," says Nancy. "Michael came with buckets of wildflower seeds, and we mixed Ted's ashes in them.

Michael gave each of the grandchildren a pail and shovel and said, 'Go where I tell you and spread them around.' The next spring, there were so many bluebonnets blooming where they'd distributed the seeds. Whenever the wildflowers come up, I feel Ted's presence."

Michael continues to be involved with plant selection and figuring out solutions when feral hogs, javelinas, tunneling gophers, and ground squirrels show up. Fencing, a driveway gate, and a perimeter planting of agave and yucca have so far deterred the hogs and javelinas. He's still working on a solution for the rodents. Alia Gunnell of West Texas Roots handles day-to-day maintenance like weeding and pruning. "It's constant upkeep," admits Nancy. But she knows why it's worth it. "It's the love of the garden. It's Ted. It's the grandchildren. I love to take my friends there. I love it so much. It's a perfect native garden that represents Fort Davis."

ABOVE: Beaked yucca and whale's tongue agave overlook a bermed lawn where Nancy's grandchildren play.

LEFT: Nancy Haywood enjoys a view of the wildflower meadow from a steel garden bench, a gift from her family.

ABOVE: Giant hesperaloe sends up 12-foot bloom spikes of creamy white flowers that are pollinated by bats. Seedpods form after flowers drop.

RIGHT: Autumn sage's tubular raspberry blossoms and minty leaves make it a garden standout.

OPPOSITE: In a rock garden along the drive, Wheeler's sotol, beaked yucca, whale's tongue agave, and ocotillo offer architectural beauty.

ABOVE: In the front garden, a rare Texas madrone displays handsome exfoliating bark and a muscular trunk.

RIGHT: The red windmill no longer pumps water but still provides ranch style.

LEFT: Lemon-yellow blossoms of perennial Mexican tulip poppy give way to long, skinny seedpods.

BELOW: Nancy's cutting garden is conveniently located just outside the much-used sunporch.

OPPOSITE, TOP: The windmill's water tank was converted into a plunge pool that the grandchildren enjoy.

OPPOSITE, BOTTOM: Blue mealy sage blossoms in the wildflower meadow.

ABOVE: A porch with a keyhole doorway shelters the entrance of the adobe-and-stone house. Yellow bells, Mexican grass tree, and bougainvillea add color and movement.

Use Boulders for Garden Seating

Large rocks are good for building up raised beds or adding naturalistic accents. They can also make a handy garden bench. Michael placed boulders throughout Nancy and Ted's meadow garden, echoing the stony cliff of Fort Davis visible across the road.

Some of the boulders hold back soil in raised beds. Others crop up amid the wildflowers in imitation of the natural landscape. Flat-topped boulders along paths make convenient spots to sit and enjoy the garden.

Waterwise Plants for a Desert Garden

1/ **Silver cholla** (*Cylindropuntia echinocarpa*): segmented stems furred with white spines display yellow-green fruits after flowers drop. 2/ **Tulip prickly pear** (*Opuntia camanchica*): round green pads with golden spines are topped with showy yellow flowers with red centers in spring. 3/ **Beaked yucca** (*Yucca rostrata*): blue-green leaves make a strappy pompom atop a shaggy trunk clothed in old leaves. 4/ **Faxon yucca** (*Yucca faxoniana*): tall trunking yucca with stiff, sword-like leaves and ivory flower clusters. 5/ **Arizona cypress** (*Hesperocyparis arizonica*): evergreen pyramidal tree with resinous, blue-green foliage and exfoliating bark. 6/ **Yellow bells** (*Tecoma stans* var. *stans*): upright, leafy shrub with abundant bell-shaped yellow flowers. This selection hails from northern Mexico.

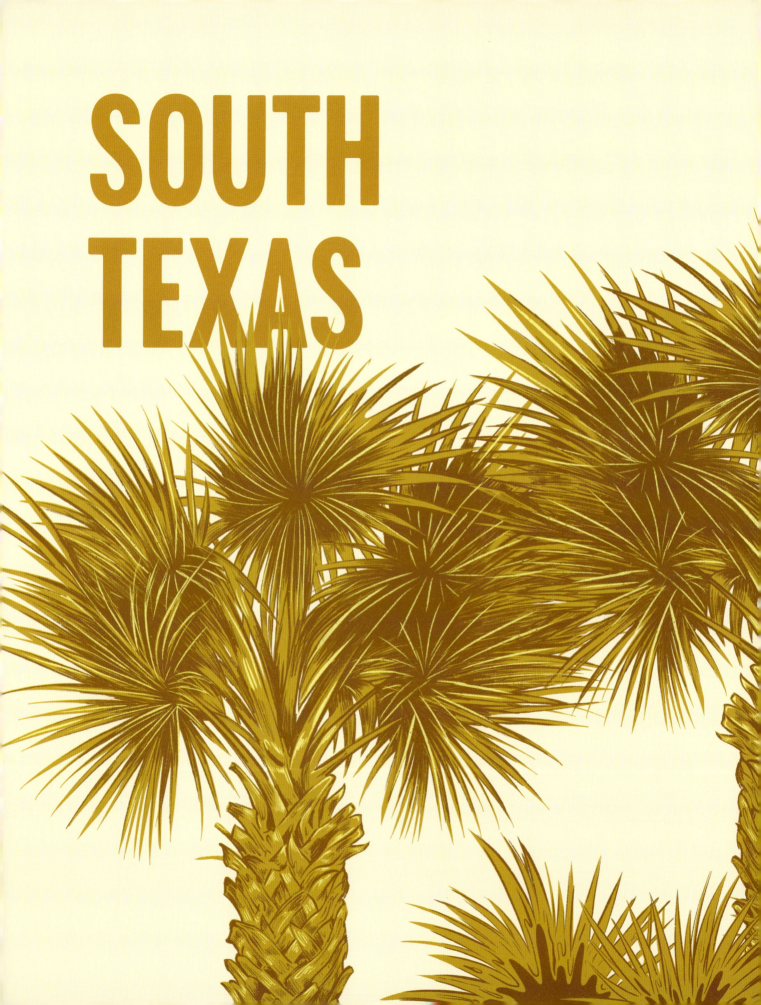

SOUTH TEXAS

THE PLACE

South Texas is a place of thorn and plains. Rolling live oak savanna flattening to spine-tipped brushland. Impenetrable thornscrub sheltering migratory birds, butterflies, ocelots, and other secretive wildlife. Palmettos shaggy with pleated-fan foliage in the delta flatland.

CLIMATE

Humid subtropical to semiarid. Summers are long and very hot, and winters brief and mild, especially in the Rio Grande Valley. Rainfall varies significantly, with a yearly average ranging from 32 inches in San Antonio to 22 inches along the Mexican border.

CHALLENGES AHEAD

Summers are growing hotter and longer, and droughts are expected to intensify. Tropical storms and hurricanes gain strength from the warming Gulf, increasing the risk of flooding, storm surges, and wind damage. Along the border, the flow of the Rio Grande, the main water source for the region, is dwindling.

TAKE ACTION

- ☐ Install gutters and cisterns to collect and store rainwater.

- ☐ Install drip irrigation, which is less wasteful and more targeted than overhead sprinklers. Drip is sometimes exempt from municipal watering restrictions because of its efficiency.

- ☐ Choose native plants, which evolved to survive the weather extremes of their native range, and well-adapted nonnatives that can tolerate record highs and lows, not just average temps.

- ☐ Remove paving where possible and plant native grasses to soak up heavy rains.

- ☐ Reduce lawn and replace with waterwise plants.

- ☐ Create shade by planting trees on the southwest and southeast sides of the garden and by building pergolas or installing shade sails over patios.

- ☐ Practice fire-wise landscaping if you live near forest or brush country.

A GARDEN MEANT TO BE

"I GREW UP literally a mile away," says Linda Peterson of her home in north San Antonio. "Before our subdivision was here, it was all wild except for one big, abandoned house that was falling down in disrepair. It had a circular driveway that ran around this batch of live oaks. My best friend and I would ride our bikes around these big trees and solve the problems of the world. They were giant trees when I was twelve, and I'm 72 now." Those majestic live oaks today stretch tentacle-like limbs across Linda's water-wise gravel garden. One tree extends an arm through a porthole in the sage green stucco wall enclosing her courtyard garden and then branches off in three directions, its questing limbs hovering a few feet above the earth. One limb rests on the ground like a supportive elbow. In the tree's leafy embrace, Linda laid patio stone and set up a rustic wooden table and stools made of tree-trunk segments.

Making her home under these trees was fated, she says. When she and husband Carl were looking for a lot on which to build a custom home, they found the property for sale, but only as a package deal with the lot next door. The young couple decided they could afford both lots if they built a house on the other lot to sell and used the proceeds to finance their dream home under the trees. They built on the other lot, but time slipped away, and they ended up raising their twin daughters there. Meanwhile the charismatic oaks next door entranced the next generation of Petersons. "When the girls were little," says Linda, "the tree that now grows through the wall had a lot of limbs that were even lower. The girls had a little cave under the limbs that nobody knew about but them. It was their favorite place. They would go out there for hours with their books, and no one would know they were there. That's how they liked it. It was my friend-tree and their friend-tree. It was meant to be."

After the girls were grown, Linda and Carl finally built on the lot—the house is their own design, and Carl handled the construction—taking care to preserve as many live oaks as possible by siting the house toward the back. That left room for a big courtyard in front. "We'd always wanted a courtyard," says Linda. "We both have Mexican backgrounds, and I have Greek, and courtyards and stucco are a thing in both places. I needed to be able to see outside from every room, but you want privacy, and that's what the courtyard is for. You can have all your views and leave your windows uncovered."

They moved into their new home in 2008, and Linda started making a garden the next spring. She'd had traditional landscaping with a lawn at the old house but found it boring. "You edge and feed and water and then do it again," she says. San Antonio's water utility was encouraging residents to conserve water by reducing lawn, and Linda was sold. "I thought, what do we want a lawn for? It didn't fit." A trip to Australia's Outback proved revelatory and inspired Linda's new garden. "We were

OPPOSITE: Whale's tongue agave gives toothy structure to a silvery mix of Gregg dalea, blackfoot daisy, Texas sage, and blue grama.

FOLLOWING PAGE: In the outer garden, xeric plants like blackfoot daisy, whale's tongue agave, Gregg dalea, blue grama, and Wheeler's sotol flourish in full sun and reflected heat from the street.

there after a rare rainy season," recalls Linda, "and the Australian desert was in full bloom. I totally felt at home. The plants are all gray-green and quirky, and they have lots of blooms, but they're funky and odd. The colors are muted and dusty. It's red but not cherry red. It's pink but not lipstick pink. I thought, this is so beautiful. This is what I want."

Linda came home and started planting without concern about fitting in with neighboring yards. "That's freeing but also scary, to have that many choices," she says. She decided to make the sunny outer garden naturalistic yet manicured, with big spiny agaves, sprawling rosemary, and trailing lantana set amid sparkling grasses and Gregg dalea, a silvery groundcover. The courtyard would be more refined and peaceful, with generous paving for sitting by an outdoor fireplace, curved planting beds along the walls, and potted olives and agaves. "I like crooked trees like oaks and olives," says Linda. "I like spiky plants. I love agaves for the contrast of big, spiky things against the walls, and I like little poofy plants like daisies growing under them. It's all about the contrast." In the back and side gardens, Linda created multiple small seating areas under the oaks with vignettes of potted plants and garden art. "Coming from a Greek and Mexican background, you always have container plants," says Linda. "In Greece, there's no ground to plant in. Everything's in olive oil cans. In Mexico it's the same thing, except they use pepper or tomato cans. To me that's natural—just without the cans." Throughout the garden, Linda spread putty-colored Texas-blend ⅝-inch gravel, and Carl laid paths and patios of greenish Pennsylvania bluestone to match the gray-green home. A menagerie of Mexican-made metal and carved stone animals, collected by the couple for decades, are tucked throughout the garden, adding quirky personality.

Lately Mother Nature has done much of the thinning that a gardener might expect to do in a mature garden. After two hard winters in a row, Linda lost her big, treasured Weber agaves and variegated American agaves. The freezes also claimed her carefully sculpted rosemary shrubs and spineless prickly pear. "The garden is very spare compared to what was there before," she says. "But I like it. I'm not bothered by more open space. It doesn't feel bare to me." A self-proclaimed clutter-hater, Linda finds the negative space calming. Fewer plants also means less maintenance, although Linda is quick to admit she still spends a lot of time working in the garden. But the plants she tends these days don't need replacing after a week of freezing temps or extended drought. "The garden in general is much grassier than it once was," explains Linda. "The grasses can withstand everything once established, and they don't require a whole lot. And they look pretty. A lot of fussier plants went away." Chartreuse bamboo muhly, fizzy 'Blonde Ambition' blue grama, and fluffy pink and white Gulf muhly grasses bend and sway in the outer garden, adding deer-resistant, veil-like texture. Toothy sotol and strappy hesperaloe are new favorites too, shrugging off extremes of both heat and cold and requiring no supplemental water to keep them green.

Although she didn't plan for it, Linda has been gardening for Texas's changing climate since day one, by selecting plants that could make it on their own in a garden without an irrigation system or constant hand watering. "I chose plants the way I would choose children, if you could," she says with a laugh. Giving her plants an imaginary talking-to, she says, "You're going to have to make it on your own at some point. So man up and learn to live with what you're getting, because I'm not going to baby you." Despite such tough talk, Linda dotes on her garden and knows it's exactly what their one-of-a-kind house under the live oaks needed. "What inspired the garden was the house," she says. "This garden would not have occurred to me with any other house. It can't have a lawn. It can't have hedges. It doesn't want that. It would spit it back out. It called for this garden."

ABOVE: The courtyard garden, built around several large live oaks, offers privacy and a shady hangout space.

LEFT: Linda Peterson spent her childhood playing among the charismatic live oaks that her home and garden are now built around.

ABOVE: A few of Linda's metal lizards convene around a potted pencil milkbush.

RIGHT: A flagstone path widens along a bend to make room for a small sitting spot.

OPPOSITE: Dusty turquoise and olive green pots of succulents, foxtail fern, and banana are arranged in front of a screen of woven slats of leftover metal roofing, which Linda and Carl designed and fabricated themselves.

ABOVE LEFT: A hanging birdbath entices wildlife to drop in.

LEFT: Linda makes abstract flowers out of bendable copper tubing inserted into stems of copper pipe.

ABOVE: An octopus-limbed live oak reaches through a cutout in the courtyard wall to embrace a rustic table and stump stools.

ABOVE: A fireplace in the walled courtyard adds ambience in summer and warmth in winter for a comfortable seating area.

RIGHT: A collection of rusty lanterns and bronze pottery makes a pretty vignette on the fireplace hearth.

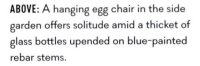

ABOVE: A hanging egg chair in the side garden offers solitude amid a thicket of glass bottles upended on blue-painted rebar stems.

ABOVE RIGHT: Vitex is one of Linda's favorite small trees thanks to its "pretty leaf shape, gorgeous blooms, wonky growth pattern, and hardiness."

RIGHT: In the courtyard, a metal rhino greets visitors near the square-windowed iron front door.

Color-Coordinate Containers

To create cohesiveness among a collection of potted plants, consider using containers of a similar hue, like Linda does. Along her driveway, sandy brown pots bring harmony to nearly two dozen plants, allowing their green and silver-green foliage to take center stage as the eye skims over their containers. Linda continues the color scheme in the brick and paver pedestals that elevate some of the pots, in the metal lizards that congregate among them, and in the finishing touch of brown river rock and broken flagstone covering the soil in the bigger containers.

Elsewhere, Linda uses dusty turquoise and olive green for her container color scheme, with pale blue beach pebbles as a finishing mulch (see page 195). The result is an eye-pleasing arrangement that reads as a whole entity, rather than a random assortment of pots.

Waterwise Groundcovers for South Texas

1/ **Lamb's ear** (*Stachys byzantina*): fuzzy, silver-green leaves make a pettable evergreen mat. 2/ **Lavender cotton** (*Santolina chamaecyparissus*): mounds of aromatic, silver-green foliage with button-like yellow flowers. 3/ **Trailing lantana** (*Lantana montevidensis*): sprawling or cascading perennial with abundant lavender flowers. 4/ **Creeping rosemary** (*Rosmarinus officinalis* 'Prostratus'): trailing, fragrant, evergreen foliage with tiny blue flowers in winter that feed bees. 5/ **Foxtail fern** (*Asparagus densiflorus* 'Myersii'): long, upright fronds of feathery foliage, evergreen in mild winters. 6/ **'Powis Castle' artemisia** (*Artemisia* × 'Powis Castle'): silver-green mound of aromatic, fern-like leaves. 7/ **Blackfoot daisy** (*Melampodium leucanthum*): white flowers with yellow centers brighten tidy mounds of narrow green leaves. 8/ **Gregg dalea** (*Dalea greggii*): spreading mass of silvery leaves with tiny purple flowers in spring and early summer. 9/ **Silver ponyfoot** (*Dichondra argentea*): creeping strands of silvery green or gray cloven leaves.

NATURE ENHANCED

OVER NEARLY 25 YEARS of working with the owners of this home in Hill Country Village, an enclave in north San Antonio, landscape architect John S. Troy has watched the garden mature through seasons of drought, heat, Arctic cold, and torrential downpours. And he's learned not to stress too much when Mother Nature throws a curve ball. "The clients have engaged me for two decades to be thoughtful about the evolution of the garden," he says, "not to think of the garden as 'one and done.' That's important. So we don't freak out over the weather. It's just nature." John's acceptance mirrors that of the owners. The husband, says John, views challenging weather events as opportunities for rethinking the garden's design. "He'll say, 'Look at how beautiful nature is and how it changes. Let's embrace this.' That philosophy has played well in the garden."

Located just ten minutes from the airport in a city of nearly 1½ million people, the property enjoys a surprisingly rural appearance, including a sun-dappled woodland along a winding drive, a glade-like backyard, woodland trails, and a sunny wildflower meadow. The plant palette consists of mostly native, rugged species that evolved in harmony with the rollercoaster weather to which South Texas has always been prone. "We always had a natural aesthetic," says John. "And we had deer. We knew horticulturally introduced plants were not necessarily going to make it, so we didn't use those." Sotol, salvia, Turk's cap, Texas sage, yucca, agarita, hesperaloe, skullcap, and various grasses thrive amid the oak, cedar elm, and juniper that were already growing here. "We wanted the house to feel it's part of the landscape, not foreign to it," adds John.

The owners hired architect Michael G. Imber to design their gabled limestone-and-stucco home, which was completed in 2003. John collaborated closely with Imber's team and the landscape contractor to integrate the house with the garden and the wilder landscape surrounding it. The original 5-acre lot was deep but relatively narrow. Dense plantings of trees and shrubs along the edges created privacy and a sense that the property extended beyond its borders. Later, the owners acquired a 9-acre parcel next door, and John began opening up the garden on that side with an extended drive for access, a wildflower meadow, and longer views.

Influenced by Frederick Law Olmsted, who designed New York City's Central Park to look effortlessly natural yet subtly amplified, John applied that philosophy to his client's property. "This is nature," he says, "but we tried to make it more beautiful. We wanted to add to it as opposed to dominate over it. We wanted to be sympatico, where the power of nature was enhanced." Those efforts begin with the driveway, which meanders toward the house through park-like scenery of mature trees and intermittent clusters of understory trees, shrubs, grasses, and perennials set off by

OPPOSITE: A faux bois bench overlooks a wildflower meadow visible through the trees.

FOLLOWING PAGE: A meadow of blanketflower is accessed via winding stone steps from the side patio.

slabs of exposed limestone. By removing some of the existing junipers, John created pockets of sun for the naturalistic pocket plantings. "We thinned the junipers in order to open up to the light, and to have light and dark spaces," he says. "We tried to appreciate each plant for its beauty rather than saying, 'All junipers must go!'" In Olmsted fashion, John sited the driveway to take advantage of views and the natural terrain. "This is very English," he says. "You have a country home, and you bring the entry road around for a glimpse of the house. You make a question mark and then arrive at the front door. It's a slow reveal."

At the entrance, a serpentine limestone wall holds the slope and leads the eye toward the front door, which is guarded by a majestic cedar elm that was saved during construction by determined effort. An intimate side patio overlooks a lower meadow ablaze with orange blanketflower in early summer. In back, large windows and a deep screened porch enjoy views of a sinuous lawn, a swimming pool and spa, and a woodland garden where a flagstone path curves invitingly through dark tree trunks, with benches and faux bois seating placed along the way. Emerging from

the cool shade of the trees into bright sunlight at the rear of the garden, the path leads to a vegetable and cutting garden, a gabled chicken coop, and a charming stone shed. From here, a mulched woodland path wanders on through a wilder portion of the property.

For John, after a quarter-century of involvement in the garden's evolution, what satisfies him most is its sense of retreat from the outside world, its self-sufficiency, and its embrace of nature—even nature at its most challenging. "The effect of climate events has not changed the overall style of the garden," he says. "It's just changed some of the plants we use." After an extended deep freeze in 2021 killed some screening trees and shrubs, John and his clients spotted an opportunity to lighten the mature, plant-heavy garden. "I said, 'Hey, we filled that up with plants, but now it's a nice negative space. So let's put something low in there, like Turk's cap, rather than a big shrub,'" he recalls. As freezes and droughts have made their mark, "We've opened the garden up to have more of a sense of reveal and closure and reveal," says John. "We took it as an opportunity and not as, 'Oh my gosh, the world is over.'"

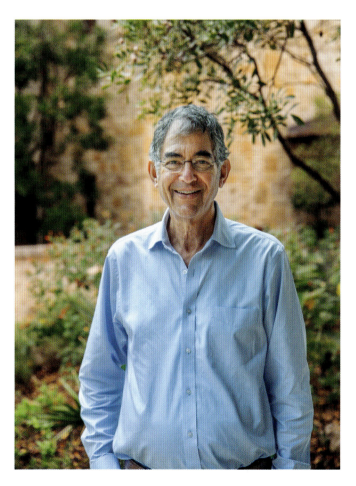

ABOVE: A screened porch enjoys a backyard view of a grilling patio, curvy lawn, and live oaks underplanted with shade-loving perennials and small trees.

LEFT: Landscape architect John S. Troy has been working with the owners on the garden for nearly 25 years.

OPPOSITE: Hesperaloe and blue nolina were planted around an existing Texas persimmon, creating the sense of a landscape that just grew naturally.

ABOVE: A potted rose of Sharon displays pink-and-burgundy flowers in the fenced vegetable garden.

RIGHT: A handsome, peak-roofed henhouse keeps the owners' backyard flock safe.

OPPOSITE: A flagstone path winds through a grove of live oaks toward the pool patio.

ABOVE: Scuppers spill water from the spa wall into the swimming pool. A blue nolina adds a starburst of blue-green foliage.

RIGHT: Mexican hat wildflowers add early summer color to a grassy meadow.

RIGHT: In the vegetable garden, limestone-edged raised beds contain a mix of edibles and flowers.

BELOW: 'Mystic Spires' salvia and flowering yucca brighten a woodland edge.

OPPOSITE, CLOCKWISE FROM TOP:
At the front of the house, a tall cedar elm shades a bed of Turk's cap, agarita, Texas mountain laurel, and dwarf palmetto.

Blue nolina adds strappy texture and height along the driveway wall.

A Charles Umlauf sculpture of St. Francis of Assisi makes a focal point along a path.

ABOVE: Clustered native shrubs and perennials make naturalistic pocket gardens along the winding driveway.

Enhance Nature

Those blessed with a larger property must often husband their resources—time, money, water—by landscaping around the house and leaving the rest wild. Sometimes, though, this can lead to an abrupt transition between the garden and wilder areas. By selectively editing and planting, you can smooth this transition and blend the two. John and the owners of this property took this approach along the driveway that winds through a wooded area to the house.

John selectively removed Ashe junipers along the drive to open up pockets of sunlight. Boulders of native stone were brought in to build up gently curving beds, which he filled with drought-tolerant native shrubs, grasses, and perennials including agarita, Texas sage, hesperaloe, and muhly grasses. The result looks like Mother Nature could have planted it, but with subtle amplifications: clusters of evergreen shrubs to screen views and flowering plants for seasonal color. It's nature, but an enhanced, idealized version that blends with the lusher main garden around the house.

Plants that Blend Cultivated and Wild

1/ **Texas sage** (*Leucophyllum frutescens*): silver-green leaves get a jolt of violet flower color when humidity rises before or after a rain. 2/ **Pink skullcap** (*Scutellaria suffrutescens*): evergreen, ground-hugging foliage is covered with rose pink flowers from spring through fall. 3/ **Blanketflower** (*Gaillardia pulchella*): annual wildflower with showy, red-and-yellow-rayed blossoms. 4/ **Prickly pear** (*Opuntia* spp.): evergreen, flat, round pads that may be spineless or bristling with golden spines. 5/ **Turk's cap** (*Malvaviscus arboreus* var. *drummondii*): spiraling crimson flowers, held above crinkled green leaves, are a hummingbird favorite. 6/ **Agarita** (*Berberis trifoliolata*): holly-like evergreen with prickly leaves, yellow flowers in late winter, and red berries that feed birds and other wildlife.

TERRA PRETA FARM

"WE ALWAYS WANT TO KNOW who's growing our food and how they're doing it," says Shakera Raygoza. It turns out that the best way to know that has been to grow it themselves. Back when Shakera and husband Juan were starting their family, they wanted to put healthy, organically grown food on their table. Unfortunately, fresh organic food was hard to find in their community, and they lived in an apartment with no place to plant a garden. A friend with a yard offered them space for vegetable plots, and soon Shakera and Juan were harvesting more than their own family could eat. Encouraged, they took their surplus to local farmers' markets to sell. "It seemed like something that could produce a side source of income," recalls Shakera. "It's just grown from there."

Fifteen years later, Juan and Shakera have three kids, a couple of farm dogs, goats, chickens, and a 20-acre certified organic farm in Edinburg in the fertile Rio Grande Valley. The busy couple works full time at other jobs, Juan as the director of the Beginning Farmer and Rancher Development Program at UT Rio Grande Valley, and Shakera as the director of the nonprofit Sentli Center for Regenerative Agriculture; she also works with the National Young Farmers Coalition to help young farmers access USDA programs. They run the farm on the side with a few part-time helpers, producing tomatoes, peppers, eggplants, okra, cabbages, radishes, beets, broccoli, cauliflower, lettuces, and more. The farming season in the Valley, which rarely sees a freeze but broils in summer, is "the opposite of up north," says Shakera. "We start harvesting in November, and we finish up in June."

In the early years, the couple sold their produce at markets and as a community supported agriculture (CSA) farm. Today they sell mainly to wholesale customers while also contributing to veggie boxes sold to local subscribers. Giving back to their community by sharing the farm is important to them too. They open to school groups for tours, to university students doing research, and to customers who want to harvest their own food or flowers from designated plots. "Hopefully we can have more open-farm events," says Shakera. "Right now, we're working with Sentli, a nonprofit I started during the pandemic. We're going to start offering classes here at the farm, like how to prepare food, how to start gardening, things like that."

Juan and Shakera were reading a book on soil fertility when they learned about *terra preta* (Portuguese for "dark earth"), uber-fertile pockets of black soil in the Amazon Basin built up by the practices of indigenous people one to two thousand years ago. Inspired, they named their farm Terra Preta, and they continually work on improving its soil, seeing soil fertility as the basis of successful organic farming. Juan, who grew up in Mexico, has a master's degree

OPPOSITE: Chard is one of the nutritious greens that the Raygoza family grows on their farm.

FOLLOWING PAGE: Terra Preta Farm is a 20-acre certified organic farm in the Rio Grande Valley.

in plant and soil science. Shakera, a Florida native, didn't know anything about farming before they started their family farm. "But Juan had the background," she says. "With hands-on experience and by reading and visiting other farms, we learned how to grow in this region." Still, farming is a nonstop learning curve. "You think you've got it down, and something changes," she says. "It's very stressful at times because there's a lot of risk in farming. When it's full season, we have to be out there every day, planting or weeding or controlling pests, and when we get a crop, harvesting and packing. And then hoping and praying that everything gets sold."

Farmers have always been at the mercy of Mother Nature, but climate change has brought more extreme heat and drought, stronger hurricanes, and unexpected freezes, like the one in February 2021 that battered Texas all the way down to the Rio Grande Valley. "That was a hard one," says Shakera. "We lost quite a few acres of radish." To adapt, they're planting warm-season crops later—"we used to plant in January, and now we wait until end of February," she says—and choosing species that are more heat and drought tolerant. She and Juan also installed high

tunnels—long plastic hoop houses—to protect crops from hail and extend the growing season.

In 2022, Shakera testified in front of the U.S. House of Representatives Committee on Agriculture about the impacts of climate change on small farmers and how USDA safety-net programs could be made more accessible to BIPOC (Black, Indigenous, and People of Color) farmers, who often face unique barriers in accessing these programs. "It was my first time speaking," says Shakera. "I was pretty nervous, but we practiced, so I wasn't *as* nervous." Shakera spoke about which programs work well and which don't, and about the need for technical support for small-scale farmers who are already stretched thin or who lack knowledge about available programs, in order to get lengthy applications for grants or claims filled out correctly and on time. She hopes that her testimony will lead to more support for young BIPOC farmers like herself and Juan, who are eager to sustainably grow food for their communities while adapting to a rapidly changing climate.

As Shakera and Juan raise their children—Shakera, 17; Kanani, 14; and Andres, 10—on the farm, they're teaching them where their food comes from, from seed to harvest. The kids pitch in when they're not too busy with school activities. "They mostly help with the animals," says Shakera. "Once or twice a year they'll help with seed planting. Andres shows the most interest. He loves to plant seeds and tend to little trees and shrubs." As the family has grown, the farm has grown and become a vital part of the Rio Grande Valley. "We farm to always have a source of food and to grow for the local community," says Shakera. "Farming should be grounded in community. It works better with a lot of support."

ABOVE: A small flock of Cinnamon Queen chickens provides eggs for the family.

LEFT: Juan and Shakera Raygoza and their children, Andres, Shakera, and Kanani, make Terra Preta a family enterprise.

OPPOSITE: The Raygozas grow a few rows of flowers for pick-your-own bouquets.

ABOVE: Pepa the goat earns her keep eating weeds. "The goats are basically pets," says Shakera.

RIGHT: Juan moves a crate of produce with his tractor.

OPPOSITE: Shakera packs radishes for market.

OPPOSITE, CLOCKWISE FROM TOP LEFT:
A flock of birds flies over the farm.

Shakera holds a hand-lettered sign
for Terra Preta Farm.

Genovese basil, a sweet basil with large,
flavorful leaves and a spicy fragrance,
is one of the farm's fall crops.

ABOVE: Bananas screen the road
and produce fruit.

Grow Your Own Food

Shakera and Juan began growing vegetables to provide healthy, organic food for their family. You can too. Here are tips for making your own homegrown farm.

» **LOCATION** Choose a sunny spot unshaded by trees or buildings. Don't feel you must hide a vegetable garden in a corner of the backyard. The center of the yard—even the front yard, if HOA rules don't prohibit it—can often be the best spot, with lots of sun (at least six hours per day) and easy access. Siting the garden near a hose spigot makes watering more convenient.

» **SIZE** It doesn't take much space to produce more food than you can eat. Start small but leave room to add more planting beds if you decide to grow more. Beds are typically 3 by 6 feet or 4 by 8 feet, which utilizes standard lengths of lumber. Space beds far enough apart so taller plants won't shade smaller plants in an adjacent bed.

» **BUILD UP** Make raised beds to ensure good soil and drainage. The simplest way is to mound a row of organic matter (leaves, grass clippings, pine straw) 4 to 6 inches deep, and top that with 6 to 8 inches of garden soil. Or build a raised bed—1 to 3 feet high is typical—to make planting, weeding, and harvesting easier. Use rot-resistant cedar, stacked stone, cinder block, or steel to edge the raised bed, or purchase ready-made planters or stock tanks (remove drain plugs and add drainage holes). Fill to the top with good garden soil slightly mounded, as soil will settle over time. Water deeply to moisten the soil, and wait a day before planting.

» **PLANT** Some vegetables are easily grown by seed, the most economical option. Others are better transplanted as seedlings from the nursery. In Texas, vegetable gardening is typically done in spring and fall, with a break during the hot summer. A winter garden is doable too for cool-season veggies.

» **WATER** Use soaker hoses or drip irrigation to evenly water and avoid wetting leaves, which can lead to foliage diseases. If watering by hand, water gently but deeply enough to reach the roots. The frequency will depend on rainfall, your climate, and growing instructions for your crops.

» **WEED AND CONTROL PESTS** Check regularly for weeds and pull them while they're small. Avoid using herbicides in an edible garden. Keep an eye out for pests, and consult local resources for information on managing them.

» **HARVEST** As vegetables ripen, harvest daily. Eat and enjoy!

Fall-Planted Crops for the Rio Grande Valley

1/ **Cherry tomato:** sweet, small round tomato. Plant transplants mid-September through mid-October. 2/ **Kale:** nutritious leafy green with ruffled foliage. Plant transplants early September through early December. 3/ **Beefsteak tomato:** large, meaty tomato that ripens to red. Plant transplants mid-September through mid-October. 4/ **Cilantro:** pungent, peppery herb used in Asian and Mexican cuisine. Plant transplants early October through early February. 5/ **Red chard:** leafy green with bright red stems and veins. Plant transplants mid-October through mid-February. 6/ **Red round radish:** root vegetable with peppery, sharp flavor. Direct-sow seeds mid-September through late October. 7/ **Genovese basil:** traditional, sweet-tasting herb used in Italian cuisine. Plant transplants early August through early November. 8/ **Zucchini:** mild-flavored summer squash. Plant transplants mid-August through mid-September. 9/ **Slicing cucumber:** crisp, refreshing vegetable for salads or snacking. Direct-sow seeds mid-August through mid-September.

TREEHOUSE RAVINE

"WE LIVE IN A TREEHOUSE in the middle of San Antonio," says Dacia Napier of the home she and husband Lanham built in the embrace of a half-dozen heritage live oaks. "The trees are the most important part of this property." The granddaddy of them all stretches a great sinewy limb over a second-story porch and reaches for the glass-walled, upper-level living room while executing a balletic backbend. Its canopy shades the swimming pool deck and softens the house. "The house that was here before was centered on this giant oak tree," says Dacia, "and now our house is centered around the tree. It's an oasis."

Despite the magnificent trees, the 3-acre lot was less an oasis and more an eroded ravine, devoid of an understory, when architect Tobin Smith began designing the Napiers' contemporary copper, limestone, and glass home in the mid-2010s. Tobin recommended the couple bring in Christy Ten Eyck, principal of Austin-based Ten Eyck Landscape Architects, to overhaul the landscaping. Dacia already had a kind of English garden in mind. "I wanted flowering plants," she says. "I like bees and butterflies and birds and color. I also wanted low maintenance because it's a lot of property." She had done a little gardening at her previous house, trying out various plants, but native plants and a waterwise landscape weren't at the top of her wish list. "Xeriscaping in my mind was always cactus and gravel," recalls Dacia. "I didn't want to do that. I wanted it to look green and lush.

But from Christy, we learned native plants are not just cactus and gravel."

For Christy, the top priority was safeguarding the grand old oaks, which included keeping their extensive root zones unsmothered and allowing water and air to reach them. "The property had great trees," she recalls of her initial visit, "but it had no planting underneath. It was all about protecting the trees and bringing the native shade understory back." In the front yard, Christy specified water-permeable paving for the circular driveway to let rainwater soak into the soil. And where the yard falls off steeply downhill, she planted masses of sedge, sea oats, and dwarf palmettos to slow runoff, giving it time to percolate to tree roots. In back, she filled out the missing understory with Texas redbud, Texas mountain laurel, Turk's cap, river fern, white mistflower, American beautyberry, and other shade lovers. And instead of funneling drainage in a buried culvert pipe, she "surfaced" a wet-weather creek, which the house straddles, giving celebratory prominence to the ephemeral path of water as it flows around the pool and through the garden.

Water makes another focal point in a grotto-like space at the back of the house. "Dacia wanted a water feature," says Christy,

OPPOSITE: Berkeley sedge, bamboo muhly, and whale's tongue agave make a textural, evergreen tapestry in the front garden.

FOLLOWING PAGE: The swimming pool and spa overlook the ravine's wet-weather creek and naturalistic garden.

"and we had the idea to do an A/C condensate pipe dripping into a steel square, which feeds into a koi pond." The pure water of the condensate is supplemented, as needed, with water from a well on the property. "We have a well for watering, so we aren't taking city water," says Dacia. "And with our native plants, we don't have to water as much. It makes a big difference." The pond quickly became one of Dacia's favorite spaces in the garden, in part for the wildlife it attracts. "Every time I come home from a trip, the first thing I do is walk into the backyard to see what's changed," she says. "I check on the koi pond and see if there are any turtles or frogs. At night we get frog music and fireflies. Frogs will be doing their thing, and then there will be thousands of eggs in the pond." Dacia also enjoys the seasonal changes of the garden, from the early spring race between redbuds and Texas mountain laurels to be the first to bloom, to the quiet dormancy of plants after a freeze. "I like the whole process," says Dacia.

Avid collectors of contemporary art, the Napiers display a handful of outdoor works in the garden, including a 2-D blue light bulb by Michael Craig-Martin and floral sculptures by Ernesto Neto. In the 2 acres at the rear of the property, the couple installed trails that meander through the trees. For their children, Cade and Avery, who were in their tweens at the time, they added wooden treehouses, swings, and a zipline. "During COVID," says Dacia, when everyone was isolating and public parks were closed, "I had a sign-up list, and neighbors could come use it as their own private park for their family." Dacia's longtime gardener, Jorge Salazar, maintains the play equipment and trails and manages the rest of the garden's care.

As the garden has matured over the past decade and weathered drought, punishing heat waves, and extreme cold, Dacia has been impressed by the resilience of its largely native plant palette. "In February 2021, it froze here for a week," she says. "Everyone on the street lost the majority of their landscaping except for us. We lost some smaller bushes in the back, but not much." Dacia trusts that native plants will ensure the garden's survival even in the face of climate challenges. "Climate 'change' sounds benign," she says, "but volatility is really what it is. We've had freezes with a week of snow, and just a few weeks later it was hot. And the summer heat has become so extreme." She feels protective of the garden and the big old trees that they inherited. "You can buy a new tree, but it's not the same as an older tree," she says. "We're stewards not only of this property but of the garden we put in. It's a living thing. I have to take care of it."

With its charismatic live oaks, leafy understory of native plants, and rugged slash of a wet-weather creek running through the center, the garden has transformed Dacia's feelings about what a beautiful garden can be. She no longer pines for a blooming English garden and urges others in South Texas to give natives and waterwise gardening a try. "Don't buy into xeriscape as being an Arizona desert with gravel and a cactus," she says. "That's not what a native plant garden is here. Here, it's making sure you use plants that can handle our weather volatility, that can make it on their own, that don't need tons of water. You can still have a beautiful, lush garden with a lot of variety and flowers and wildlife. You can still have it all—it's just a different all. It's not an English garden, but I think it's as enticing as any peonies."

ABOVE: In a ferny grotto under the main level of the house, a steel-cube pool collects air-conditioning condensate that drips from a suspended pipe. Bronze branches with porcelain flowers by artist David Wiseman adorn the wall.

LEFT: Dacia Napier was happy to learn that a garden of native and adapted plants can be lush and green.

ABOVE: Landscape architect Christy Ten Eyck brought the wet-weather creek to prominence, rather than funneling runoff through underground pipes, to celebrate the path of water.

RIGHT: Star-shaped whale's tongue agaves cluster in a grassy swath of Berkeley sedge.

OPPOSITE: A live oak stretches its great limbs over the pool deck and makes the contemporary home feel like a treehouse.

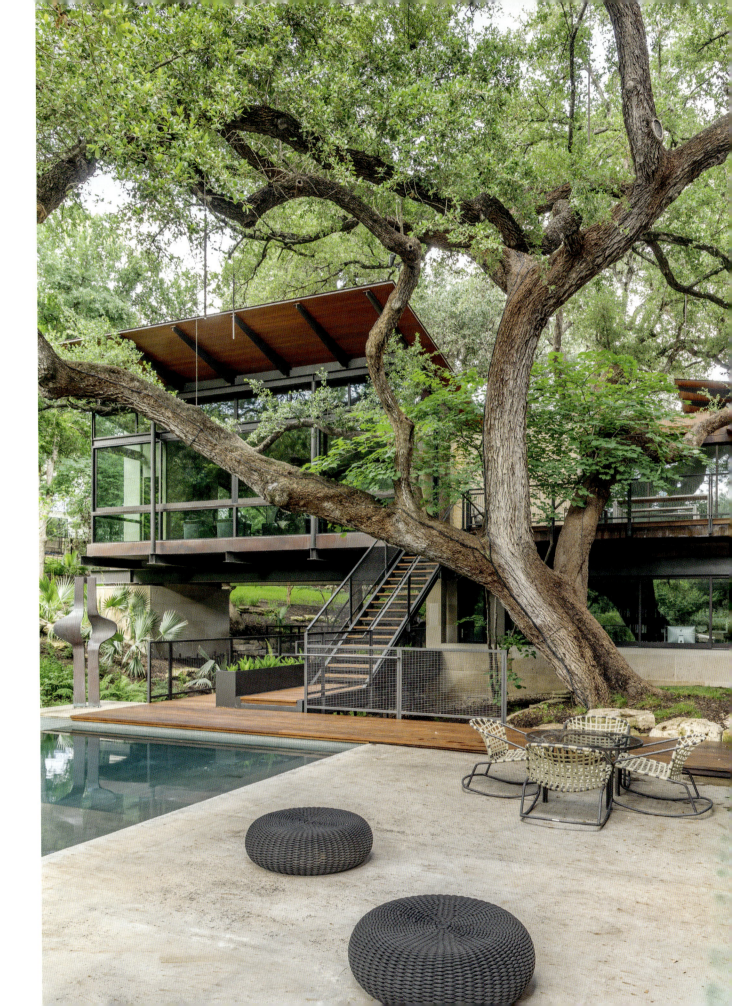

ABOVE: Shade-loving inland sea oats makes a grassy groundcover in the front garden.

LEFT: A rill spills water across rock ledges into a koi pond. Colocasia, sedges, and ferns colonize the moist edges.

RIGHT: River fern glows in the sunlight.

BELOW: Beyond the negative-edge swimming pool, dwarf palmetto displays fan-like leaves, underplanted with feathery coralberry.

LEFT: A blue light bulb sculpture by Michael Craig-Martin adds a surreal element to the garden.

BELOW LEFT: Delicate lavender flowers of American beautyberry ripen in autumn into clusters of bright purple berries, a favorite of birds.

BELOW: A steel-edged rill funnels water from the cube water feature into the koi pond.

OPPOSITE: Turk's cap, Texas redbud, and dwarf palmetto fill the leafy understory.

Go Waterwise Beyond Cactus

Xeriscaping, aka water-conserving landscaping, can get a bad rap. For some, the term conjures an image of a hot, rocky yard accented with cacti and a cow skull. That wasn't the look Dacia was going for when she hired Christy to design her garden. She wanted green abundance, and she was delighted to learn that a garden of largely native plants can be waterwise *and* green and lush. Here are ways of making a water-conserving garden that go beyond river rock and cactus.

» **PLANT SHADE** Add one or more trees on the southwest side of your yard to provide shade from the hot afternoon sun. Tree shade helps soil retain moisture and can provide as much as 10 to 20 degrees of cooling.

» **REDUCE IMPERVIOUS COVER** Choose porous paving—water-permeable pavers (like Dacia's driveway), unmortared flagstone, gravel—instead of a solid expanse of concrete or asphalt. This allows rainwater to reach tree roots and hydrate the soil instead of running off into a storm drain.

» **SLOW RUNOFF** Cover bare soil with plants to create a dense layer of foliage that slows runoff, giving soil and roots time to soak up water (except in desert gardens, where open space between plants is a natural water-conserving adaptation).

» **RIGHT PLANT, RIGHT PLACE** Match plants to the conditions in your yard for healthy plants with less need for irrigation. For Dacia's front garden, Christy chose a mix of native and well-adapted plants that thrive in the shade of live oaks, like whale's tongue agave, Berkeley sedge, pale-leaf yucca, silver saw palmetto, and giant leopard plant. Elsewhere, Turk's cap, dwarf palmetto, and inland sea oats fill the understory of the wetter ravine.

Understory Plants for South Texas

1/ River fern (*Thelypteris kunthii*): graceful lime-green fronds make a slowly spreading, feathery groundcover. **2/ Inland sea oats** (*Chasmanthium latifolium*): leafy, clumping grass with flat, drooping seedheads that start bright green and ripen to tan. It seeds out readily and makes a good choice for erosion control. **3/ Silver saw palmetto** (*Serenoa repens*): fan-shaped, silvery blue leaves with sharp teeth along the stems. **4/ Whale's**

tongue agave (*Agave ovatifolia*): wide, cupped, blue-green leaves tipped with mahogany spines, with good tolerance for bright shade if given good drainage. **5/ Dwarf palmetto** (*Sabal minor*): evergreen, fan-shaped leaves with excellent cold and heat tolerance. **6/ Berkeley sedge** (*Carex divulsa*): evergreen, meadowy clumps that slowly knit together for a lawn-like effect.

GARDENING IN MEMORY

WHEN SUZANNE WARE MOVED to Texas from Indiana—"the land of flowers and lots of rain," says her daughter Sarah Ware Fielden—she planted peonies and calla lilies, envisioning a lush, flowery garden at her new home. The plants failed in San Antonio's torrid summer. So Suzanne pivoted, looking to Italian gardens for inspiration. "My mom spent a lot of time in Europe, and she always thought of this as a little Palladian villa," says Sarah of the family compound her parents, Denny and Suzanne, bought in 2000. "It has that Italian influence. Mom wanted more flowers in the summer, but it's so hard to have them here. If she couldn't have that, she wanted an evergreen garden—palms, boxwood. She wanted to have life in the garden year-round. And here, you *can* have that."

Suzanne took classes to learn about gardening in South Texas's humid subtropical climate and became certified as a master gardener. She also began creating an Italian-inspired garden to complement the limestone-and-stucco house designed by San Antonio architect Don B. McDonald. The garden is formally laid out with creamy limestone walls, stairs, and terracing. Hardy evergreens like Texas palmetto, boxwood, and cast-iron plant glow in shades of green amid the sinuous black trunks of live oaks. Sinewy arbors and trellises constructed from native cedar ground the garden firmly in Texas, as do locally crafted faux bois seating, a sculpted limestone deer, and a Texas-flag art cow purchased at a fundraising auction for the American Cancer Society. "My dad has always loved Texas and had cowboy boots as long as I can remember," says Sarah. "Everyone joked that he was all hat and no cattle. Now he has a cow." Denny also contributed an elegant circular fountain with limestone coping, sited on axis with the front door. Set in the lawn amid a dozen live oaks, their dark trunks like calligraphy brushstrokes, the blue pool with arcing jets of water has a fairy-tale quality. "My dad wanted the fountain," says Sarah. "It's a showstopper, and he loves it. The lawn was the most logical place for it. Mom loved her trees. She didn't want to take any trees down, and they could put it there without losing any trees except cedars."

On the other side of the house, alongside the driveway, Suzanne installed a terraced boxwood parterre with a small patio in the center. A faux bois table and chairs, with a bark-like finish that echoes the live oaks, provides a spot to sit. A monumental trellis constructed of cedar posts runs the length of the parterre, visually connecting the main house to a detached garage and defining the garden room. Fig ivy traced the trellis with evergreen leaves until Winter Storm Uri killed it in 2021, but new vines are climbing the posts. Along the driveway,

OPPOSITE: A clipped boxwood ball is illuminated by late afternoon light under sinuous live oaks.

FOLLOWING PAGE: A terraced boxwood parterre includes an intimate patio in the center. Along its length, a cedar grid makes a rustic, windowed separation between the garden and a tree-studded lawn.

A romantic fountain splashes amid gnarled live oaks in the lawn below the house.

a dry creek manages runoff, and a meadowy swath of Mexican feathergrass provides movement and texture. Near the swimming pool, potted amaryllis and beds of lily of the Nile and bear's breeches offer seasonal flowers.

Suzanne enjoyed sharing her garden with friends and family, including her six children and numerous grandchildren, says Sarah. In 2017, Suzanne opened the garden for a public tour benefitting the Garden Conservancy, one of her favorite charities. Two years later, following a long illness, Suzanne passed away. Sarah has been maintaining her mother's beloved garden ever since. Residing in the guesthouse that overlooks the garden, Sarah has a daily connection to her mother's memory. "I always felt very close to my mom," she says, "and I got a lot of strength from that. Taking care of the garden was hard in the beginning, and I tried to do it to honor her because I know how much she loved it. I felt a responsibility to take it on. And I understand her better now because I know why she loved it so much. I learned what beauty it brings."

Suzanne's longtime gardener, Ramiro Sanchez, and his assistant, Mago Arvizu Palacio, continue to maintain the garden and the 10-acre grounds on a full-time basis. "They are both fantastic," says Sarah. "I could not do this without them." Like her mother before her, Sarah enjoys walking in the garden and looking for what's growing or blooming. "There are still new surprises to this day, things that I haven't noticed before, and something blooming almost every month of the year," she says. For a time, Sarah felt she needed to keep the garden looking exactly as her mother had left it. But as she's grown in confidence and knowledge, she's begun to make a few changes. "We used to have lily of the Nile in two beds," she says, "but it only bloomed on one side because it got sun there. On the other side it didn't. I decided to pull up the shady side and move it where it gets sun. It may sound silly, but that was a hard decision. But I knew the plants would thrive better down there."

By tending her mother's garden, Sarah is growing into a gardener herself. She thinks about her mom when the pompom lily of the Nile flowers appear; when the toothy leaves of bear's breeches return after summer dormancy; when tiny Lady Banks roses cascade from canes arching into the trees; when the wisteria on the arbor dangles fragrant blossoms in early spring. The garden is a tangible connection. They are gardening together through memory. "When I do things and add different things," says Sarah, "I think, would Mom enjoy this? Would she think it's the right decision?" She pauses, mentally takes stock of their garden, and answers her own question. "I think she's looking down and thinking I'm doing a good job."

ABOVE: Live oaks shade a limestone-edged fountain and swimming pool. Gravel terraces adorned with potted amaryllis and boxwood invite relaxation.

LEFT: Sarah Ware Fielden learned to care for the garden to honor the memory of her mother, Suzanne Ware, who created and cherished it.

ABOVE: The guesthouse opens onto a gravel terrace with an Italian ambience.

RIGHT: Faux bois chairs and a table echo the trunks of live oaks that shade the terrace.

OPPOSITE: Bear's breeches flowers in late spring and then goes dormant during the hot summer.

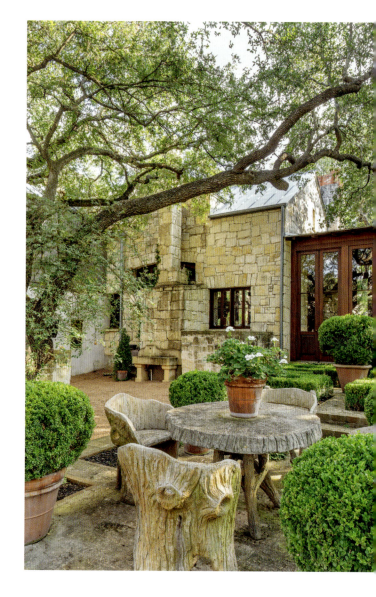

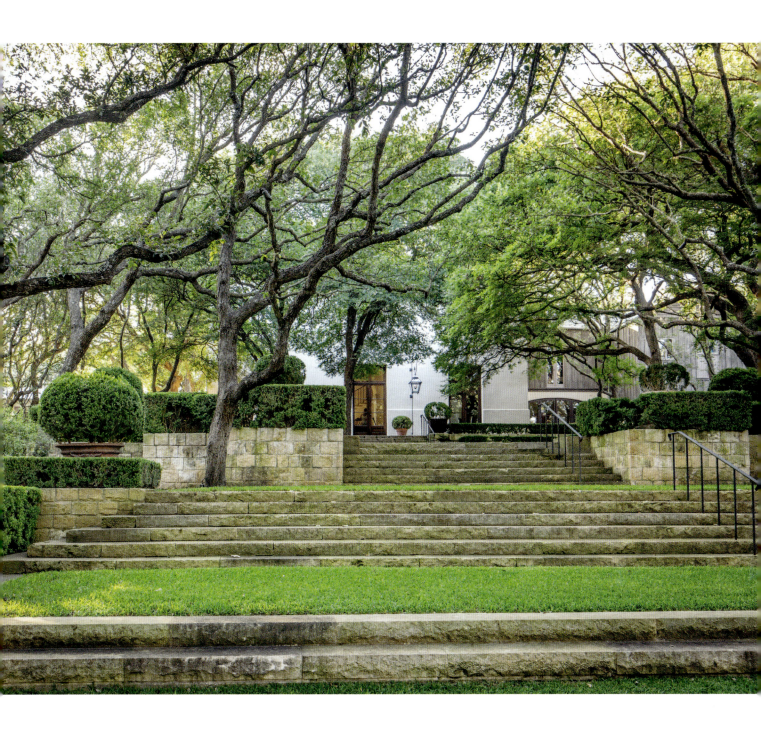

OPPOSITE, TOP: A Texas-flag art cow adds humor to the garden and reflects owner Denny's appreciation for all things Texan.

OPPOSITE, BOTTOM: A shady wisteria arbor leads to a sunny gravel terrace with potted boxwoods and pelargonium.

ABOVE: Limestone stairs elegantly terrace a slope, greened up with boxwood hedges and potted boxwood balls.

ABOVE: Texas palmetto, cast-iron plant, liriope, and boxwood green up the garden year-round.

RIGHT: A limestone stag carved by Fredericksburg sculptor Russ Thayer—one of a pair on the driveway's gateposts—symbolizes the property's name of Deerfield.

ABOVE: A majestic Texas palmetto is underplanted with lily of the Nile and potted boxwood.

LEFT: Fluffy Mexican feathergrass makes a low-water groundcover.

Embrace Place with Local Materials

To give your garden a distinct sense of place that celebrates the region you call home, use locally sourced materials and furnishings. Suzanne selected rustic elements—cedar posts, faux bois, and chunky blocks of limestone—to ground her elegant garden in the rugged natural landscape of San Antonio.

» **CEDAR POSTS** A long wisteria arbor and a monumental trellis grid made of sinewy cedar (also known as Ashe juniper) posts create shade and screening.

» **FAUX BOIS** Suzanne's faux bois benches, chairs, and table are examples of local artistry, part of San Antonio's century-old tradition of *trabajo rustico*, which translates to "rustic work." Made of concrete crafted to look like tree trunks, branches, and sawn wood,

the art form originated in Europe, made its way to Argentina, and from there traveled up to Mexico and San Antonio.

» **LIMESTONE** Early settlers in San Antonio found limestone in abundance and quarried it to build their homes and businesses. The garden's use of limestone around the swimming pool and fountain, and in walls and steps, evokes the region's architectural history.

South-Meets-South Texas Plants

1/ Lily of the Nile (*Agapanthus africanus*): strappy, glossy evergreen leaves and globe-shaped blue or white flower clusters from late spring to early summer. **2/ Cast-iron plant** (*Aspidistra elatior*): evergreen shade lover with dense clusters of upright, sword-shaped leaves. **3/ Texas palmetto** (*Sabal mexicana*): slow-growing but eventually tall native palmetto with woody, cross-hatched trunk and fan-shaped leaves. **4/ Boxwood** (*Buxus microphylla*): evergreen shrub easily shaped into globes or hedges. Susceptible to boxwood blight, so choose with care or substitute dwarf yaupon holly for a similar look. **5/ Live oak** (*Quercus fusiformis*): long-lived, handsome tree with undulating limbs and nearly evergreen canopy. Protect from oak wilt by pruning only between July and January, using disinfected tools, and by immediately painting cuts. **6/ Bear's breeches** (*Acanthus mollis*): large, glossy, notched foliage may go dormant in summer but reappears in fall. Tiered mauve-and-white flower spikes add spring color.

THE PLACE

North Texas is a place of grasses, wind, and woodland. Copper grasses bowing beneath the wind's steady caress. Purple wands of gayfeather waving above a scrim of muhly and little bluestem. Rugged belts of post oak and blackjack oak segueing to wildflower-dotted savanna.

CLIMATE

Humid subtropical. Summers are long and hot, and winters are mild, although hard freezes can be expected. Wind is a steady presence, and spring storms may spawn tornadoes. Rainfall occurs throughout the year, with an annual average of between 35 and 40 inches.

CHALLENGES AHEAD

Summers are growing hotter and longer, and droughts are expected to intensify. Rainfall may remain at similar levels but fall with increased intensity, leading to more runoff and flash flooding. Winters will be warmer overall but may bring more extreme cold snaps.

TAKE ACTION

- ☐ Install gutters and cisterns to collect and store rainwater.

- ☐ Install drip irrigation, which is less wasteful and more targeted than overhead sprinklers. Drip is sometimes exempt from municipal watering restrictions because of its efficiency.

- ☐ Choose native plants, which evolved to survive the weather extremes of their native range, and well-adapted nonnatives that can tolerate record highs and lows, not just average temps.

- ☐ Add rain gardens to manage runoff. Install terracing or check dams on slopes to hold rainwater and give it time to soak into the soil.

- ☐ Create shade by planting trees on the southwest and southeast sides of the garden and by building pergolas or installing shade sails over patios.

- ☐ Plant a prairie garden instead of lawn, where appropriate.

- ☐ Practice fire-wise landscaping if you live near forest or grassland.

PLANO PRAIRIE GARDEN

"I GROW A BUNCH OF WEEDS," says Michael McDowell of his garden, alight with sun-catching grasses and tall purple wands of gayfeather, which stands out amid the neatly mown lawns on his suburban street. "To most people, that's what it is," he explains. "Or that's what they think it is. If they see it at the right time of year, they might change their minds about it." Changing people's minds about what a front yard should look like, and offering a radically different alternative, has been a sort of side gig for Michael since 2009, when he launched a blog about his garden called Plano Prairie Garden. It quickly developed a devoted readership. Nowadays he shares his garden on Instagram, where he garners hundreds of likes for videos of monarchs fueling up on Gregg's mistflower and images of his lawn's transformation into a garden of native prairie plants.

When he bought his red-brick ranch in Plano twenty years ago, he inherited a "pretty basic" landscape: lawn with a line of shrubs along the foundation and a dying peach tree in back. A lifelong gardener, Michael soon dug out the back lawn so he could plant the antique roses and other plants he'd brought with him from his previous garden. "Then I got more into natives," he says, "although at the time they were kind of hard to find." Out came the roses. In went tall prairie grasses like switchgrass and Indian grass. But when the tidy 1-gallons he planted grew to 5 feet across and began spreading, he reconsidered. Nowadays he corrals a few of these big grasses in stock-tank planters to soften the back fence, while in the garden proper he favors smaller grasses, particularly pine muhly and little bluestem, which match the scale of his small lot.

Eventually Michael turned his attention to the front yard, and once again the lawn got the shovel. He began his blog at the same time, mainly, he says, to document publicly that his no-lawn landscaping was intentional and not due to neglect. "If anybody complained," he recalls thinking, "I could point to the blog and all these pictures and naming plants and say, 'I'm not lazy. There's a purpose here.'" Ten years on, a sense of purpose still drives Michael's plant choices. He's not gardening just for himself, he says, but for birds, insects, and other wild creatures that need food and shelter. "I try to find plants that have a dual purpose, whether for pollinators or as a host plant for caterpillars or with berries or seeds for birds." These native grasses, annuals, and perennials, which once thrived in wild abundance on the Blackland Prairie before it was tilled for farmland and subdivisions, fill Michael's garden and attract local and passing-through wildlife. On sunny early October afternoons, the garden seems to vibrate with bees gathering pollen and monarch butterflies nectaring on mistflower and gayfeather. Many of his neighbors appreciate the wildlife activity too. "A lot of the neighbors walking by say they like coming here, and they bring their kids and point out

OPPOSITE: Michael's garden is a stopover for migrating monarch butterflies.

FOLLOWING PAGE: Texas gayfeather's purple flower spikes put on a show in early October.

butterflies and bees," says Michael. "One family calls it the butterfly house."

When he started making his prairie garden two decades ago, many native plants were viewed as weeds, and it was hard to find them at nurseries. Michael had to sleuth out new species to try. "There were a couple nurseries that sold some," he says, "and I became aware of the Native Plant Society of Texas sales. Here in the Dallas area, there are a few chapters, and I'd hit all of those. I'd buy one or two of each plant to see if it would survive or try to take over. If it was well behaved and lived, it would probably set seed or I could divide it, and I'd end up with more plants." Over time he selected for the natives that performed best and grew more of them for a cohesive effect. "All of the gayfeather in the front yard started with one 4-inch pot that had two plants in it," he says. "I planted one plant at each end of the yard. After they bloomed, I scattered their seed, and in a few years it pretty much filled in. It got to a point where I was cutting seeds off before they hit the ground so I wouldn't have too many. But it's a good plant because it ties everything together and creates a uniform appearance, instead of having 50 different kinds of plants out there."

While Michael acknowledges that maintaining his garden requires a lot more time and effort than it would to mow a lawn, he takes satisfaction in the wildlife oasis and plant diversity he's made room for

on a small suburban lot. The mostly native garden also requires very little water, even after a blisteringly hot and dry summer. "I usually won't water at all until August or September," Michael says. If the garden gets a little crispy during the summer, it rebounds when rain does come, and the whole garden bursts into bloom just in time for the monarch migration in early October. "I primarily use water-conserving plants," Michael says. "There was a time when we had a bad drought and were on watering restrictions, and my yard looked pretty good without any water. Native plants for the win!"

Now that his garden is mature, Michael finds he's having to remove more plants than he adds, partly to make maintenance easier as he ages and partly because some plants have outgrown their location or attracted pests. Recently, tired of raking up leaves and acorns from a red oak he planted years ago, he cut it down, opening his back garden to full sun again. In front, he yanked out several large prickly pears that were continually infested with cactus bugs. He's unconcerned about losing such structural plants—what some might call the bones of the garden—and he follows his intuition when it comes to design. "I get an urge and follow through," he says with a laugh. "I'm trying to make it easier. Maintaining the garden is not as easy on me as when I was ten years younger. I want to still have and enjoy the garden when I'm 80 and be able to take care of it."

By removing woody plants, Michael is essentially restoring his garden to grassland, and doing what fire and bison grazing accomplished before the Blackland Prairie was converted to farmland. "I kind of miss the cactus," Michael says with a touch of wistfulness before remembering an unexpected upside. "But one thing I don't miss is that when people would visit, because of the cactus, they would always say my yard reminded them of Arizona or New Mexico. That was not my goal. These are Texas plants. It's supposed to remind you of Texas."

ABOVE: Pine muhly's airy stems poke up amid gayfeather flowers.

LEFT: Michael McDowell propagated many of the prairie plants in his garden by collecting seed and spreading it around.

OPPOSITE: A bee collects pollen on tall boneset's white flowers.

ABOVE: Clammyweed's beanpod-like seed capsules are held like raised arms.

RIGHT: A birdbath in the back garden sustains not only birds but pollinators too.

OPPOSITE: The tiny yellow flowers of prairie broomweed sparkle amid gayfeather's purple wands.

ABOVE: A bird's-eye view reveals that Michael's garden is an oasis of color, texture, and wildlife habitat amid suburban lawns.

LEFT: Pale-leaf yucca's upright, blue-green leaves add evergreen structure to a prairie garden.

BELOW: Little bluestem's fluffy seeds incandesce in the afternoon light.

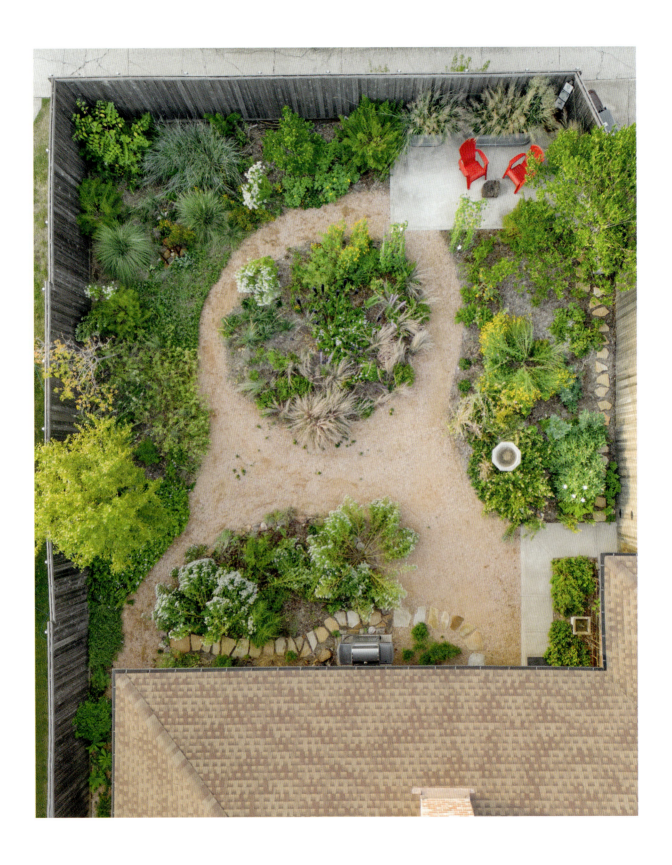

ABOVE: Little bluestem, mistflower, and tall gayfeather surround a bottle bush Michael made by bending long pieces of rebar and pushing them into the soil.

LEFT: Cowpen daisy and long stems of Indian grass beautify a small patio in the back garden.

OPPOSITE: In the no-lawn back garden, a decomposed granite path encircles an island bed. Michael retained an existing concrete pad for stock-tank planters and a seating area.

Grow Plants from Seed

When you're on a budget or simply can't find enough of the plants you want, give seed sowing a try. Propagating your own plants from seed saves money, and it's rewarding to observe a plant's complete life cycle. Here are a few of Michael's tips.

» **OBSERVE BEFORE SOWING** Before collecting seed and spreading it around, Michael trials new plants to make sure they're a good fit for his garden. He purchases one or two plants of a particular species, plants them in different spots, and observes. "I never know if a native plant will survive in my conditions, or if it will have ambitions to take over," he says. A trial period gives him that info.

» **WAIT FOR SEED TO RIPEN** If a new plant thrives and he wants more of it, Michael waits for its flowers to go to seed and ripen. Then he collects the seed and scatters it wherever he wants more plants. He generally follows nature's timing and sows seed as he collects it. But sometimes he holds back a handful of seed for scattering later, in the fall, which he feels increases the odds of germination.

» **SOWING IN POTS VS. IN THE GARDEN** Get a jump on spring by sowing seeds in pots and keeping them in a heated greenhouse or indoors under grow lights until after your last frost date, when it's safe to transplant them into the garden. For Michael, sowing in pots is more work than he wants to do. But if you want to try it, first research to see if your seed-bearing plant is suitable for sowing in pots. Some plants are, but others grow better when directly sown into the garden.

» **TRANSPLANT VOLUNTEERS** Seedlings that pop up on their own are called volunteers, and they can be a great source of free new plants. Michael often finds volunteers growing in his decomposed granite paths. He carefully digs them up and transplants them where he wants them, boosting his collection. Watch out, though: weed seedlings love decomposed granite too, so learn to distinguish baby weeds from wanted seedlings, and dispose of the former.

» **LEAVE SOME SEED** As you harvest seed, leave some on plants that birds depend on for food in fall or winter, particularly sunflower, coneflower, salvia, and grasses.

Prairie Plants for North Texas

1/ **Texas palafox** (*Palafoxia texana*): annual with pink, fringy flowers on slender, branching stems. 2/ **Plateau goldeneye** (*Viguiera dentata*): tall, bushy perennial with golden flowers that feed birds in winter. 3/ **Gregg's mistflower** (*Conoclinium greggii*): fuzzy periwinkle flower clusters attract butterflies galore in fall. 4/ **Little bluestem** (*Schizachyrium scoparium*): small, upright grass with fine foliage that starts out blue-green and ripens to reddish bronze with fluffy seedheads. 5/ **Clammy-weed** (*Polanisia dodecandra*): annual with white flowers with pink stamens, slender seedpods, and sticky leaves that give it its common name. 6/ **Texas gayfeather** (*Liatris punctata* var. *mucronata*): showy purple flower spikes in fall attract bees and butterflies. 7/ **Pale-leaf yucca** (*Yucca pallida*): spiny blue-green leaves and a bloom spike of bell-shaped white flowers in spring. 8/ **Pine muhly** (*Muhlenbergia dubia*): attractive small grass with a spherical form, diaphanous stems, and tan seedheads. 9/ **Tall boneset** (*Eupatorium altissimum*): tall, branching perennial with clusters of small, white, fuzzy flowers.

A GARDEN FOR WALKING

DAVID ROLSTON DOES NOT OFTEN sit still in his garden. "I wake up and walk in the garden," he says. "I come home for lunch and walk in the garden. I walk at night. I walk all weekend. I enjoy it." For more than 30 years, David has been walking his half-acre garden in the historic Lakewood neighborhood of Dallas and sculpting a Texas version of an English landscape garden. Here, between expansive beds anchored by towering trees, a serpentine lawn offers an emerald invitation into the garden. Russet-leaved Japanese maples, flowering shrubs and perennials, bold-foliage annuals like castor bean, and masses of groundcovers fill out the understory. At the rear of the garden, an airy arbor of rusty steel shelters a firepit patio overlooking a round fishpond on one side and circular sunken garden on the other.

"I grew up in Iowa," says David, "which is a very pastoral landscape. My parents loved gardening, and their love for gardening influenced me." As a teen, David got his first paid gig as a designer, creating a garden for his high school art teacher's new house. "That garden still exists today, much to my chagrin," he says. "It was a young person's idea of landscape, but it was very fun." David's affinity for art, gardening, and design led him to pursue a degree in landscape architecture at Iowa State University. By 1985, having relocated to Dallas, he'd established his own firm, David Rolston Landscape Architects.

When David and wife Julie Cohn, an artist and jewelry designer, first saw their home, they were drawn to its location atop a hill, with a view of surrounding parkland near White Rock Lake. The backyard was a blank slate—"grass from stem to stern," recalls David—with skinny beds around the perimeter. As he considered what the garden should be, the property's topography held the key. "We had a 9-foot drop from the house to the lower part of the yard," he says. "I wanted to make the garden feel like it flowed down and had a sense of life to it. The land flowed, and I followed with the design." As it turned out, more than the land flowed. Whenever it rained, runoff turned a low spot at the rear of the property into a lake. Rather than funnel it into the parkland or neighboring properties, David made innovative use of the runoff. "I put in an underground reservoir under the lawn," he says. "It holds about 1200 gallons, and it can be pumped out for irrigation. It's not a lot, but it does recharge, and it saves water." A curved stone wall on the downhill side of the sunken lawn helps retain runoff, giving it time to soak through the soil and into the retention system.

David's knack for creative adaptation extends to plant selection too. Having grown up gardening in the famously fertile soils of Iowa, David soon learned that many familiar plants fail to thrive in Texas. "The good, basic, tough

OPPOSITE: Cascading pink flowers of 'Little Volcano' bush clover combine with the fall foliage of understory trees to brighten David's garden in autumn.

FOLLOWING PAGE: Deep, curved beds beneath the trees frame a long view toward the rear of the house.

plants that you can have in Texas may not be all the plants that grow so fabulously in the Northeast or you see in gardening books," he says. "You have to adjust to Texas and what we can have. What I do is, I just make the tough plants work." David opts for tried-and-true plants with variations in foliage color and texture instead of relying on flower color or trying to keep ill-suited plants going with chemical fertilizers or pesticides. "I don't want the risk of chemicals," he says. "And I'm too lazy to do it. I believe that a garden that has variations of color and texture and repetition is the key, and you don't have to have a high-maintenance garden to have an interesting garden. That can be achieved with tough, hardy plants that you repeat all over the place: Turk's cap, salvias, grasses, sedges. Oakleaf hydrangeas, which we have fabulous success with."

His appreciation for plants that don't need babying came, ironically, from a desire to become a father. "I used to spend 25 to 30 hours a week gardening," admits David. "But in 2000 we decided to adopt our daughter from China. Julie thought I would dump all the child-rearing duties on her and be an obnoxious gardener like I'd been for so long. She said, 'I'm not going to agree to adopt unless you agree to co-parent with me.'" David took stock of the garden and replanted much of it to make it less needy, ripping out his high-maintenance annuals and fussier perennials and replacing them with native and other hardy plants that he chose for foliage interest. With the redesigned garden requiring less of his time, David and Julie welcomed their daughter into their lives. Later on, David added spaces for child play in the garden, like a circular wading pool in a back corner. When his daughter outgrew the pool, he converted it into a pond for goldfish and water plants. These days, he and Julie enjoy sitting on their screened porch with picturesque views of the garden on all sides, or

by the firepit under the arbor. "We have to die in this house," jokes David, "because Julie won't ever give it up. She gets a lot of inspiration for her jewelry designs from the garden—from the plants, the flowers, the seedheads."

Twenty years ago, an attic fire in their home caused so much smoke damage that David and Julie had to undertake a gut renovation. In the process, they gave their 1940s colonial home a more contemporary look. David added modern accents in the garden as well, like a rectangular steel arbor framing an axis view near the screened porch. "One thing about modern landscape design is it works well with a soft English garden," says David. "I juxtapose features and elements that are a little more stark and modern with the soft, flowing things of an English garden. The tension of that feels comfortable."

Weather extremes in recent years are influencing David to make other changes. "In the past, plants were more reliable," he says. "There weren't that many surprises. Now that the climate is so erratic, I'm reorienting toward hardier plants. I'm deciding that some plants aren't going to make it through the winter." But such calculations are just part of gardening, he adds. "It doesn't mean your garden has to fall apart just because you get frustrated with the weather. Even if a plant dies, it's a new opportunity." What makes a garden survive over the long run, he says, is the gardener's own critical eye in assessing what's working and what isn't and adjusting as necessary. "My garden is 30 years old, and I do things continually. I trim this, I move this, I pull this out. It's the horticultural editing that makes a garden fresh and alive and a pleasure, as opposed to tired and overgrown and abandoned. True gardeners don't mind errors and mistakes and walking through the garden and saying, 'Next year I will do that differently.' There's always next year."

ABOVE: A round fishpond with bubbling fountain overlooks a steel arbor sheltering a firepit patio.

LEFT: David Rolston designed the steel arbor, which has a wood-plank platform on top. Accessed by a steel ladder, it offers a high view of the garden.

ABOVE: American beautyberry dazzles in fall as berries ripen to bright purple.

RIGHT: Effervescent seedheads of 'Heavy Metal' switchgrass look like fireworks going off.

OPPOSITE: A copper vessel fountain draws the eye to the end of a long path.

RIGHT: Morning glory scrambles up a contemporary steel arbor that frames an axis view.

BELOW: The garden flows downhill to a circular lawn. A reservoir beneath the lawn collects runoff, which can be pumped out for irrigation.

TOP: A focal-point potted American agave languidly extends spiny leaves.

ABOVE: A round pot of ivy makes a centerpiece for a secluded sitting area with round-backed benches and a curved screening fence.

ABOVE: A potted agave under a large tree draws the gaze across the garden.

OPPOSITE, TOP: The leaves of a Japanese maple turn rusty orange in fall.

OPPOSITE, BOTTOM: Annual castor bean has bold, reddish foliage and unusual spiny seedpods.

Make Garden Rooms

David fills deep beds with shrubs, small trees, and perennials to delineate distinct garden rooms in his half-acre garden. Within those rooms, chairs and benches offer destinations for sitting and enjoying the different views. Counterintuitively, because the entire garden can't be seen all at once, it feels even bigger. You can scale this idea to almost any size garden. Garden rooms foster a feeling of mystery—*what's around the bend?*—that entices you to walk and explore.

» **PLANT DIFFERENT USES** Consider how you'd like to spend time outdoors—for example, gathering with family around a firepit or escaping for a while to a hidden nook.

» **PUT UP "WALLS"** Once you've decided where those rooms will be located, make "walls" to create separation. You can plant a hedge, put up a trellis, or plant deep beds for screening, as David does. Even a small tree or a few shrubs can function as a divider, simply by obscuring the everything-all-at-once view.

» **LEAD ON** Access your rooms via inviting pathways, whether of lawn, flagstone, or a combination. The invitation to walk your garden will be irresistible.

Room-Defining Shrubs & Small Trees for North Texas

1/ **'Little Volcano' bush clover** (*Lespedeza thunbergii* 'Little Volcano'): large arching shrub with cascading pink flowers from late summer to fall. 2/ **Japanese maple** (*Acer palmatum*): graceful understory tree with attractive leaves that turn red, orange, or gold in fall. Many varieties and sizes are available. 3/ **American beautyberry** (*Callicarpa americana*): shade-loving deciduous shrub with arching branches bearing clusters of glossy purple berries in fall, which birds love.

4/ **Japanese plum yew** (*Cephalotaxus harringtonia* 'Nana'): slow-growing, spreading evergreen for shade with bright green new growth and shaggy texture. 5/ **Oakleaf hydrangea** (*Hydrangea quercifolia*): large leaves and showy clusters of white flowers in spring, which hang on and turn caramel-colored in fall. 6/ **'Needlepoint' Chinese holly** (*Ilex cornuta* 'Needlepoint'): glossy evergreen leaves and red berries in winter that attract birds.

PUNK ROCK GARDEN

THE SOUNDTRACK MAY BE birdsong, the humming of bees, and splashing water, not thrashing metal, but the garden that Michael and Lorie Kinler have made over the past twenty years has a punk rock spirit. "It's anti-establishment," Lorie says of their lawn-free front yard, naturalistic beds of native and other Texas-tough plants, space-defining primary-color walls, culvert-pipe planters of bamboo, and "hillbilly swimming pool." Their garden stands out with a certain punk-hairdo spikiness in their east Fort Worth neighborhood of tidy front lawns. The couple, who met in landscape architecture school and are the principals of Kinler Landscape Architecture, have been bucking mainstream ideas about what a garden should look like since they got into the business.

"When we first started designing gardens, in Dallas especially, they loved their azaleas," says Lorie. "Dallas is farther east than Fort Worth, but it's not Tyler," where acidic soil and ample rain allows azaleas to thrive and they're celebrated each spring. "People would spend all this money on bed prep and amending their soil so azaleas would grow. But to me, it was so irresponsible to do that when we have plants that work great without all that extra bed prep and water." Shunning chemical fertilizers and pesticides as well, the couple has gardened organically since their early years. Michael's mother, Ruth Kinler, founded North Texas nursery Redenta's Garden and ran it for 30 years, "and it was kind of a pioneer in organic gardening," says Michael. "That was the only way I knew how to garden. In general, we just don't do pest control and fertilizing." Adds Lorie, "We're lazy gardeners!"

When they first saw their midcentury ranch, built in 1957, they were smitten with its breeze-block wall and a sight line that ran all the way through the house to views of the backyard. "We were like, yeah, this is the house for us," recalls Lorie. The backyard was St. Augustine turf with Chinese photinia around the perimeter—a nearly blank slate. Michael and Lorie wanted distinct garden rooms and came up with the idea of dividing the yard into four long, rectangular sections: a covered patio for dining and lounging; a central planting bed dense with dwarf palmetto, Turk's cap, blue anise sage, 'Tropical Giant' spider lily, and snowball viburnum; a small lawn bordered by low, colorful walls for their young son to play on; and a neighbor-hiding screen of bamboo contained in half-buried sections of culvert pipe. As trees grew taller, they shaded the lawn so much it struggled to grow, so Michael and Lorie replaced it with artificial turf. And when their son outgrew the play space, they added the stock-tank swimming pool for themselves, for cooling soaks in summer. Their front courtyard, enclosed by the breeze-block wall,

OPPOSITE: A steel retaining wall in the office garden frames a rock-garden planting of red yucca and beaked yucca.

FOLLOWING PAGE: A stock-tank swimming pool offers cool relief during hot Texas summers.

has zen-like serenity with a western edge. Two red chairs overlook a sunken, circular fishpond—a concrete cattle-watering tank from a ranch supply store outside of Fort Worth.

When the house next door came up for sale, Michael and Lorie bought it and turned it into their business office. Its corner lot functions as a living laboratory to trial plants for use in clients' gardens. A rusty steel retaining wall adds contemporary style and terraces a sunny gravel garden for their most dry-loving plants: a yellow-flowering retama tree, red yucca, giant hesperaloe, and beaked yucca. Shade plants hug the house foundation, and flowering perennials like native pitcher sage, 'Big Momma' Turk's cap, and purple coneflower tumble around the garden's perimeter. Lorie and Michael grow a lot of native plants and use them in their contemporary designs for clients, but they're not exclusive about it. "I don't like to get locked into purity tests about native gardens," says Michael. Lorie agrees. "We try to use natives as much as we can," she says, "but there are adapted plants that do great too."

Michael enjoys puttering in the garden on weekends. "Constantly curating is really enjoyable to me," he says. "We spend so much time in front of screens. I like to get my hands dirty and move things around." For Lorie, the enjoyment comes from observation.

"We have big sliding-glass doors and windows," she says, "so when you're sitting inside, it's like you're outside. I can always see the garden. I enjoy watching all the animals." Michael agrees that simply having a view of plants and wildlife is one of a garden's great pleasures. "We talk to clients about how looking at your garden from your house is a way of using your garden. You don't have to be outside working in it or sitting in it. Just seeing it from inside your home is a benefit."

One thing the couple doesn't miss is having a traditional lawn, which needs regular watering and mowing in the hot Texas summer. "A lot of people are sick and tired of how boring lawn can be," declares Michael. "Usually people don't even use the front lawn. It's just a big, green ornament projecting to the neighborhood that you're an acceptable family." For their clients who are willing to experiment, Michael and Lorie have been making ecologically friendly, prairie-like lawns. They start by sodding buffalograss, a native turfgrass that requires little water or mowing but is vulnerable to Bermudagrass incursion if overwatered. Then they overseed with native blue grama and love grass to make a denser turf that keeps Bermuda from creeping in. "We're going to do something like this in our office garden," vows Michael. "It's changing what a lawn is."

For Lorie, part of making a more sustainable-minded garden is simply learning to live with imperfection. "A garden is a natural, living thing," she says. "It's not going to be perfect. You're going to have weeds. You're going to have plants that die. You have to be able to go with the flow and not expect everything to be perfect all the time." It's a radical idea to some—a little punk rock even—but one that pays out in enjoyment of a garden suited to its place.

ABOVE: In the breeze-block front court-yard, a round lily pond with a fountain makes a restful view.

LEFT: Michael and Lorie Kinler see their office garden as a design and plant laboratory. Their home garden, with multiple spaces for relaxation, is right next door.

OPPOSITE: Fall aster covers itself in golden-eyed purple flowers in autumn.

ABOVE: The white flowers of variegated Spanish dagger glow against a brown shed wall.

RIGHT: A shaggy beaked yucca and yellow door greet visitors in the office garden.

OPPOSITE: Lorie and Michael found the concrete tank at a ranch supply store. They partly buried it and turned it into a pond.

ABOVE: A disco ball sparkles above the covered patio, where colorful Fermob furniture extends the home's living spaces. Michael and Lorie sawed through the original concrete pad to create the look of large pavers.

OPPOSITE, TOP: Bees adore frostweed's white flower clusters.

OPPOSITE, BOTTOM: Hot-pink flowers of gaura sway in a breeze.

Artificial Turf Dos and Don'ts

Summers in Texas are hotter than ever and water for landscaping more scarce. No wonder artificial turf is soaring in popularity among homeowners who want a lawn or low-maintenance landscaping while doing their part to save water, reduce emissions from mowing and blowing, and stop using chemical fertilizers and other lawn treatments. However, faux turf has environmental shortcomings of its own. It's a petrochemical carpet with a fairly short life span (an average of ten years is commonly reported), after which it ends up in a landfill. The particulate infill that fluffs the grass blades may contribute to microplastics in the soil and waterways. And it heats up in summer sun, adding to the urban heat-island effect.

For their own backyard, which has a small artificial lawn, and in design work for clients, Lorie and Michael have found faux turf suitable for certain uses, but not as wall-to-wall carpeting. "It is not a replacement for a large lawn," cautions Lorie. "It works better as a recreational space. I use ours for yoga, and it makes a good play area for kids or a dog run."

Here are expert recommendations for using artificial turf in the best way possible.

» **KEEP IT SMALL** Don't roll out faux turf across the entire yard. Use it sparingly, only where you need a playing or lounging surface. Elsewhere, plant climate-appropriate, wildlife-friendly plants or low-water turfgrass like zoysia or Habiturf. Living plants, unlike faux turf, help cool our neighborhoods, and they don't block ground-dwelling beneficial insects or earthworms and birds that feed on both.

» **INSTALL IN THE SHADE** Faux turf can get hot enough to burn bare feet or a pet's paws in a Texas summer, especially in full sun. Some installers recommend hosing down artificial grass to keep it from getting dangerously hot, but that defeats the purposes of saving water and reducing maintenance. Installing in shade or partly shady locations is a better solution.

» **LET TREE ROOTS BREATHE** Don't wrap faux turf around a tree's trunk or smother its root zone. Most of a tree's roots grow in the top 12 to 18 inches of soil and need access to oxygen and water. The compacted base material for faux turf prevents water and air from reaching surface roots, which can kill a tree. Keep faux turf at least 4 feet away from a tree's trunk; outside the tree's drip line (the circumference of its canopy) is even better.

» **GO GEOMETRIC** A geometric shape—rectangle, circle, or oval—looks best, says Lorie. Define it with heavy-duty steel or stone edging, set flush.

Waterwise Plants for North Texas

1/ Yellow cestrum (*Cestrum aurantiacum*): medium-sized shrub with showy, yellow-orange, tubular flowers from spring to fall. **2/ Golden thryallis** (*Galphimia gracilis*): golden yellow flowers from spring to fall and evergreen foliage except after a deep freeze, when it dies to the ground but returns in spring. **3/ Giant hesperaloe** (*Hesperaloe funifera*): upright, evergreen leaves with white threads. A 10- to 15-foot flower spike of creamy flowers may appear in spring. **4/ Mexican buckeye** (*Ungnadia speciosa*): native understory tree with soft pink flowers in spring and mahogany, three-lobed seedpods in fall. **5/ Darcy's sage** (*Salvia darcyi*): fire-engine red flowers on this upright, bushy perennial draw hummingbirds, bees, and butterflies. **6/ Frostweed** (*Verbesina virginica*): upright perennial with clusters of white flowers beloved by bees and butterflies. At first frost, stems exude water that freezes into curled ribbons of ice. **7/ Fall aster** (*Symphyotrichum oblongifolium*): masses of purple flowers in fall on low bushy foliage. **8/ 'Big Momma' Turk's cap** (*Malvaviscus drummondii* 'Big Momma'): large, leafy perennial with scarlet flowers that are bigger than regular Turk's cap, and which attract hummingbirds and bees. **9/ Beaked yucca** (*Yucca rostrata*): strappy, blue-green leaves atop a shaggy trunk.

THE KEEPERS

WHEN A BLUE NORTHER sends temperatures plummeting, prompting other gardeners to dash around throwing sheets over tender plants, Toni Moorehead leaves her linens in the closet and carries on as usual. "I don't want to protect plants in the winter," she says. "I don't want to be worried if my plants will make it. And in summer I don't want to drag hoses to water hogs. I just need easy. I want plants to work or they're outta here!" That practical streak has served her well during three decades of garden making in Grapevine, northwest of Dallas. As the owner-designer of Signature Gardens, a garden design business, Toni is always watching to see how plants hold up during freezes, heat waves, droughts, and deluges. "I don't take heroic actions to protect plants," she says. "Because there are so many plants that *do* work here, I just pick something else."

At her own place—just under a half-acre with tall, light-filtering trees, on a slope that falls away to a creek—Toni layers time-tested plants into a richly textured strolling garden. Flagstone paths meander among her collection of 33 Japanese maples, whose handsome leaves turn to gold and burgundy each autumn. Leopard plant, with round leaves shaped like lily pads, and strappy 'Tropical Giant' spider lily add glossy greenery that shines in the shade; their seasonal flowers are a bonus. The oversized, crinkled leaves of oakleaf hydrangea turn maroon in fall, a second season of beauty after spring's white flower clusters. Turk's cap, autumn sage, and summer phlox add their own red or pink flowers, drawing butterflies and hummingbirds. Ground-huggers like chocolate plant, purple oxalis, 'Pale Puma' purple heart, and ajuga knit the garden together by filling the gaps.

A fishpond fed by a gentle waterfall adds Asian style to a relaxing, arbor-shaded terrace at the back of the house. Here, Toni and husband Dile enjoy a fine view of the garden from their elevated perch. A towering 'D.D. Blanchard' magnolia—a cinnamon-and-olive-green pyramid standing 70 feet tall—draws the eye to the back corner, where an arching footbridge offers passage over a dry creek. In the center of the garden, Toni shrank the lawn to a small ovoid, making its green negative space a feature rather than an afterthought. She did the same with the front lawn, shrinking it down to a circle bisected by the front walk.

Toni grew up on a Wisconsin dairy farm with a big vegetable garden that she and her siblings helped weed and plant. "I worked the garden because that's what I was supposed to do," she says, "but it's not like I really knew anything about it." In the mid-1980s, she moved to North Texas and planted her own first

OPPOSITE: A waterfall splashes into a naturalistic koi pond, a view enjoyed from the back terrace.

FOLLOWING PAGE: A large oak— a hybrid of a red oak and pin oak, according to Toni's arborist—shades half of the back garden, where paths wind through curvy beds accented with more than 30 Japanese maples.

vegetable garden, guided by the schedule she remembered following in the Upper Midwest. "In Wisconsin, you plant vegetables on Memorial Day weekend, and that's all I knew," she recalls. "So I planted a little vegetable garden in unprepared soil on Memorial Day weekend in Texas. Epic fail!" After that early misstep, Toni became friends with a neighbor whose family owned a local garden center. "She would take me down to the nursery and talk to me about plants, and we went on the local garden tour every year," says Toni. "That's when I caught the gardening bug and started thinking about design."

Wanting more space both inside and out, Toni and Dile built their current home in 1998. Toni was excited by the blank slate of a yard and the privacy afforded by mature trees and the creek along the rear of the property. "The lot was just a horse pasture sloping down to a creek that runs into Lake Grapevine," she says. "When we stood on the property and looked down and I couldn't see anybody else's roof, I said, 'This is it.'" Toni created her garden bit by bit over the years, starting with a curvy shade bed in the lower garden. "Then we had a big, frog-choking rain," she recalls, "and it carved a creek through my new bed. I thought, 'Huh! I guess I need a creek bed where the water flows.' So I got cobblestones and made a dry creek." Working her way uphill, Toni added more swooping beds and filled them with plants with contrasting textures, colors, shapes, heights, and bloom times. "I would just stand and stare," she says. "The design would come to me that way. I would stand and look at an area until I could see a bed."

Eventually Toni started in on the front yard, expanding the simple foundation beds she'd established early on. The lawn shrank, and flagstone paths meandered. Out came the turf in the sidewalk strip along the street, and in went low-growing perennials and bulbs for colorful curb appeal. "Every year I would carve out a new bed," says Toni. As the garden matured and trees grew taller, Toni replanted much of the garden for dappled shade. Just about the time she started wondering if the garden might be "done," a big tree came down, reverting shade back to sun. Toni transplanted all that she could and replanted for the new conditions. "I had the illusion that it would all just be maintenance someday," confesses Toni, "that everything would be planted where I wanted it, and all I would have to do is go around and snip-snip and tidy up. But that is not how it is, because trees continue to grow and shade beds out, or a tree falls down, and all of a sudden you have sun again. It's ever-changing. Here I am, 25 years in, still changing things. It's never done. And that's part of the awesomeness of the garden."

Over the decades, Toni has observed all kinds of weather extremes in her garden, including the historic drought of 2011, the wettest year on record in 2015, and the weeklong Arctic freeze in 2021. "Anything in my garden today has survived all of that," she says. "So these plants are keepers. I always tell people, just look at what's working in your yard and do more of it. Let's not reinvent the wheel." Toni has no interest in zone pushing, and she heeds the advice of longtime gardening experts about which plants survived past disasters. As a design professional herself, she wants to make wise recommendations for her clients and views weather extremes as a testing ground for plants. "When we were at -2°F, I didn't cover a thing," she says. "I wanted to know what was going to make it. I appreciate the extremes because it weeds out the wimps. My plant palette is getting smaller, but it's tougher."

ABOVE: Autumn daffodils, crocus-like bulbs, pop up in fall to brighten the curbside strip.

LEFT: Toni Moorehead prioritizes plants that thrive without interventions from her. "I don't like fussing with stuff," she says. "I want to put it in the ground, and it works."

ABOVE: Toni shrank her front lawn to a small circle divided by the front walk. Other paths make curving ambles through the garden.

RIGHT: A towering 'D.D. Blanchard' magnolia thrives in the moist soil of the lower garden.

OPPOSITE: A footbridge crosses a wet-weather creek that keeps runoff from eroding the sloping garden.

ABOVE: 'Red King Humbert' canna blazes alongside pink phlox and red Turk's cap in the entry garden.

RIGHT: A heron statue watches over the koi pond.

RIGHT: Anoles benefit the garden by dining on grasshoppers, crickets, roaches, and other insects.

BELOW: A path threaded with dwarf mondo grass winds through shade-loving Japanese maples, Turk's cap, holly fern, and purple oxalis.

CLOCKWISE, FROM TOP: A Chinese pistache shades part of the front garden, which Toni filled with low-growing shade lovers.

An urn fountain's shallow basin on top makes it easy for birds to bathe.

The muscular, cinnamon-colored trunks of a crape myrtle add beauty year-round. Refraining from lopping off the tops of the branches in winter—a common but misguided practice known as "crape murder"—yields this result over time.

ABOVE: The back lawn has been shrunk to a curvy swath in the sunniest spot, surrounded by deep beds of Japanese maples and other plants that appreciate some shade.

LEFT: An iron leaf holds water for birds, lizards, and pollinators. Sprinkling Mosquito Bits—a pet- and wildlife-safe biological control for mosquitoes—into standing water keeps mosquito larvae from hatching.

Go All In with Groundcovers

In Toni's garden, shade-loving groundcovers add rich texture and color along paths, between paving cracks, under trees, and around rocks. While they may not attract as much attention as a graceful Japanese maple or flowering shrub, these unassuming, low-profile plants earn their keep by knitting the garden together into a lush, cohesive scene. Here's what else they do.

» **PREVENT WEEDS AND EROSION** Like wood mulch, groundcovers blanket bare soil, which helps prevent weed seeds from germinating. Think of a groundcover as a living mulch that you don't have to spend money on to reapply every year.

» **UNIFY THE GARDEN** Groundcovers fill the gaps between larger plants, preventing the sparse look of dotted shrubs in a sea of brown mulch.

» **GREEN UP THE SHADE** Where trees make shade, turfgrass can suffer. Rather than fight it, replace shaded-out grass with a shade-loving groundcover.

» **REDUCE MOWING** Groundcovers are a good choice for a hard-to-mow slope, around trees and boulders, and anywhere you don't need or want to mow a lawn.

» **ADD TEXTURE AND BEAUTY** Best of all, groundcovers offer another layer in the garden for you to add a sweep of color, texture, and flowers.

Shade-Loving Groundcovers for North Texas

1/ **Leopard plant** (*Farfugium* sp.): gleaming round leaves and yellow, daisy-like flowers in late fall. This petite variety, perhaps a hybrid, appeared in Toni's garden years ago, and she collects and spreads its seeds to grow more. 2/ **'Pale Puma' purple heart** (*Tradescantia pallida* 'Pale Puma'): rubbery, purple-and-green leaves with a compact, creeping habit for part sun. Thrives in full sun too. 3/ **Chocolate plant** (*Pseuderanthemum alatum*): unusual chocolate-colored foliage with a jagged silver stripe and violet flowers in summer. Rarely found in nurseries,

this passalong plant is easily grown from seed shared by others. 4/ **Purple oxalis** (*Oxalis regnellii* 'Triangularis'): deep purple, triangular leaves and dainty pink flowers in spring on a diminutive clumping plant. 5/ **'Catlin's Giant' ajuga** (*Ajuga reptans* 'Catlin's Giant'): indigo flower spikes in spring above ruffled, bronze-green, ground-hugging leaves. 6/ **'Katie' dwarf ruellia** (*Ruellia simplex* 'Katie'): clumping, spreading perennial with tapered green leaves and lavender, petunia-like flowers.

HOME ON THE GRANGE

"GARDENING IS NOTHING but experimenting," says Patrick Boyd-Lloyd. "Your neighbor could have the best tomatoes, and you try that variety and get maybe 10 percent of the crop, and you think, 'What did I do wrong?' Or the opposite: you get more than they do. There are failures and challenges, but when you *do* get it right, or something good you didn't even expect, that's the joy of gardening."

For two decades, Patrick has been experimenting in his half-acre garden in the Ravinia Heights neighborhood of Dallas, figuring out what will thrive in rocky soil, under tall trees, and on a slope that drops 15 feet from one corner of the lot to the other. Despite the challenging conditions, the land is what drew him to the 1913 foursquare home he shares with husband Tom. "The trees, the natural beauty, the grade change," says Patrick. "I could see so much potential in it." Today the garden unfolds as a journey, with curving paths to encourage exploration, and with multiple destinations—an intimate porch, a spacious deck, a cozy firepit patio, and a pergola-wrapped dining arbor with fireplace—screened by an understory of perennials, shrubs, and Patrick's collection of around 30 Japanese maples. "We call the garden Ravinia Grange," he says. "The *grange* part comes from Great Britain and means a gentleman's farm."

A lifelong Dallasite, Patrick started out in fashion design but always had an interest in architecture. "As a kid, I didn't draw cartoons. I drew floor plans," he says drily. In his 30s, as a homeowner with his first garden, he learned about landscape architecture and was intrigued. "By the time I got this house," he says, "I'd started working for David Rolston Landscape Architects," where he's a senior designer today. Patrick drew on his design expertise to remake his home's entrance. Initially, the front walk ran arrow-straight from the busy street to the front-porch steps—a charmless conveyor belt of an entrance. Patrick relocated the front door to the side wall of the porch, hiding it from the street. He added more mystery by replacing the straight walk with a broad, oval path that encircles a scrim-like grove of trees and small shrubs and leads elliptically to the porch.

For paving, Patrick salvaged, from landscaping job sites, slabs of broken-up concrete, thereby diverting material from the landfill and creating a flagstone effect. A modernist gate of welded pieces of rebar, inset into an arbor, welcomes visitors at the street. Outside the gate, tufts of Mexican feathergrass in the paving and a streetside planting of whale's tongue agave, trailing lantana, salvia, dwarf ruellia, iris, and purple heart immerse visitors in the garden from the get-go. Once inside the gate, a choice must be made: right or left along the oval path? Audibly drawing visitors toward the door, a low square fountain with water splashing over

OPPOSITE: A cascade of sedges, including white-edged 'Feather Falls', flows along steps of recycled concrete.

FOLLOWING PAGE: The lushly planted garden under a canopy of trees nearly hides the two-story house from view. In the sunny lower garden, a narrow lawn makes a serpentine path leading deeper into the property.

black pebbles aligns with the gate and porch steps, helping to complete the garden's first journey of discovery.

In the lower garden, a serpentine lawn flows past terracing walls and specimen maples. Small statuary and a bowl fountain appear along the way, presenting invitations to slow down and look around. In the back corner, a minimalist arbor—just four cedar posts joined by three beams—defines a dining patio paved with bricks recycled from old chimney flues. "We've had Thanksgiving dinners there," says Patrick. He designed and fabricated a contemporary steel fireplace to warm the space on chilly days. It also makes a focal point from upslope, where a terraced lawn gives the couple's dogs a place to run and a fire-pit patio offers another gathering space. "We love to have friends over," says Patrick. "The firepit is always popular. It's the end of a propane tank on a metal stand I had fabricated. We bought an iron frame and Argentinian cross to grill over it. We've done lamb and other meats, vegetables, hot dogs, and s'mores." An ipe deck off the back of the house adds another hangout spot and bridges a 4-foot elevation change between the driveway and the corner of the house. "If the weather's nice, we'll sit on the deck and have wine or a cocktail," says Patrick.

After the prolonged deep freeze of Winter Storm Uri in 2021, Patrick lost a lot of screening shrubs around the perimeter of the garden. Evergreen viburnum, one of his favorites, was decimated, along with mature pittosporums and aralias. "I'd go look and just sit down and start crying," he recalls. "But it is what it is. Mother Nature's gonna do what she's gonna do. You've got to have your moment to get upset but then release and move on. That's what I did." Patrick replanted with cold-tolerant hollies like Liberty, Oakleaf, Oakland, and 'Nellie R. Stevens'. "For the longest time, I was like, 'Eh, hollies, not interesting,'" he says. "But now I think, 'You're a workhorse.' And I'm using these workhorses as our main structure for

the garden. Plants that I love that haven't held up as well—podocarpus, pittosporum, aralia—I'll maybe use a few and see. It could be 40 years before it gets that cold again."

Patrick has also figured out workarounds for the rubbly limestone he finds whenever he puts a shovel in the ground. Initial attempts to plant trees required the use of a jackhammer. He bermed up good soil for planting beds, but because of the slope, the soil eroded with each heavy rain. He ended up building terracing walls to hold the soil, using rock excavated when the yard was trenched for new sewer and gas lines. On the upside, says Patrick, "because we're on such rock, the drainage is exceptional. But the negative is, the drainage is exceptional. Soil can really dry out fast." He relies on a mix of native and well-adapted plants that thrive in dry shade, including Turk's cap, Gregg's mistflower, American beautyberry, sedges, 'Tropical Giant' spider lily, and his beloved Japanese maples.

After three decades of gardening and designing gardens in North Texas, Patrick has a few tips for new gardeners. First, he says, don't get sucked into impulse purchases at the nursery. Take a moment to look up a plant online to see if it grows well in your region. "If you buy something just because it's pretty, it won't last here," he cautions. He also advises prioritizing foundational expenses like drainage, an irrigation system, and a deck or patio. After that initial investment, he says, set out some furniture, plant little by little, and have a good time watching the garden grow. Gardening is nothing but experimenting, after all. "You've got to roll with it," he says.

OPPOSITE, CLOCKWISE FROM TOP: Along the street, whale's tongue agave, Mexican feather-ergrass, Texas sage, trailing lantana, and purple heart add texture and repetition under crape myrtles.

Repurposed bricks pave a Texas welcome near the front door.

For Patrick Boyd-Lloyd, the garden is a place for contemplation, to experiment with plants, and to host gatherings of friends.

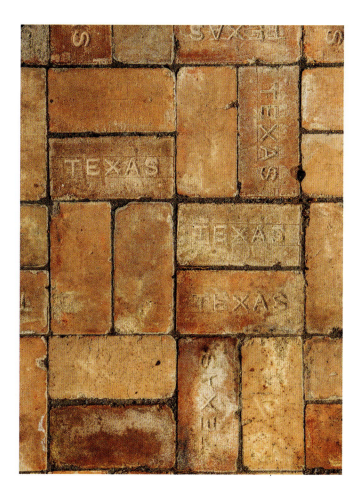

ABOVE: A low fountain along a path adds the sound of water to the dining patio and offers a drink to birds and other wildlife.

RIGHT: A dining pergola aglow with cafe lights beckons at the end of a woodland path.

OPPOSITE: An arbor with a modernist gate of welded rebar welcomes visitors. Tufts of Mexican feathergrass soften the paving.

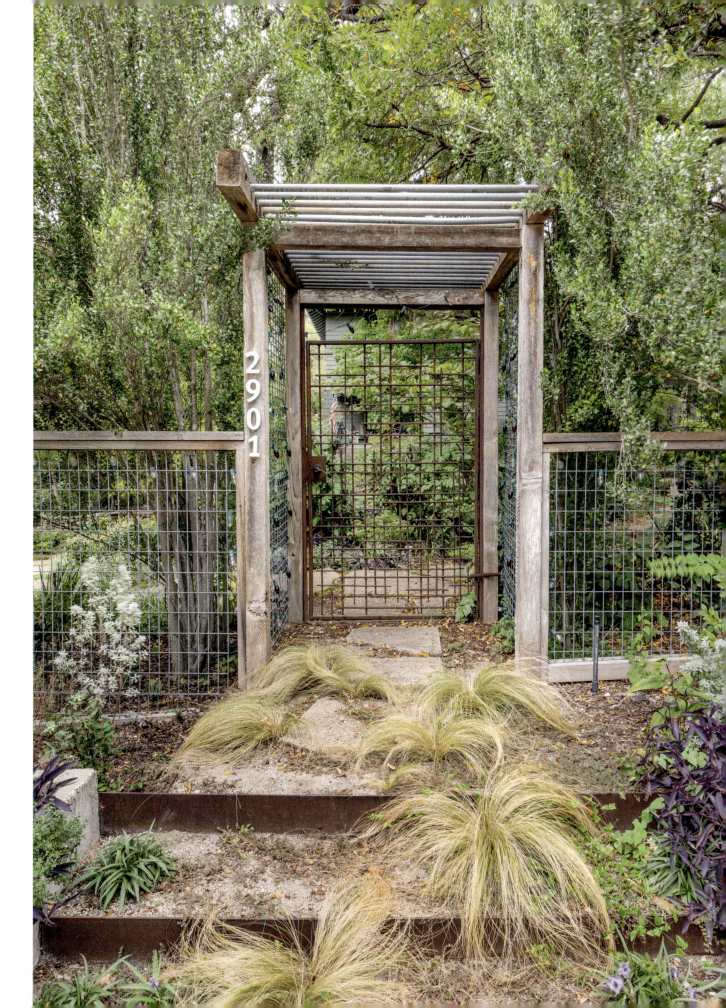

ABOVE: Patrick designed and fabricated the dining patio's steel fireplace himself. Brick from old chimney flues in the house paves the patio.

RIGHT: A small St. Francis statue graces the woodland garden.

OPPOSITE, TOP: An ipe deck spanning the back of the house is greened up with terraced garden beds and an espaliered Ebbing's elaeagnus.

OPPOSITE, BOTTOM: Chairs pulled up around a firepit make a casual gathering spot. An assortment of potted plants adds greenery and helps enclose the space.

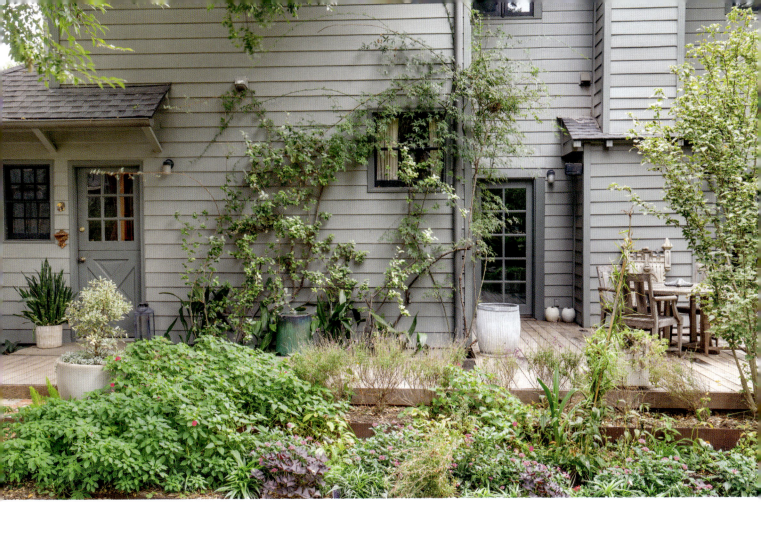

Recycle Concrete Paving

Did you know that broken slabs of concrete can substitute for flagstone? By repurposing old concrete—cheekily known as "urbanite"—you'll save money on hardscaping materials while keeping construction debris out of the landfill. Urbanite makes a durable material for paving paths and patios, building walls or raised beds, and laying steps on a slope, as Patrick did.

Make urbanite by breaking up an unwanted concrete walk or patio on your property using a pry bar and sledgehammer or a rented jackhammer. Free urbanite is often listed on sites like Facebook Marketplace, Craigslist, and Freecycle, provided you're able to haul it away. Choose flat pieces of a uniform thickness. Avoid urbanite with rebar or wire mesh sticking out of it. Larger slabs work best for patios and steps. If slabs are bigger than you need, break them into smaller pieces.

Small Trees and Shrubs for North Texas

1/ **Coral bark Japanese maple** (*Acer palmatum* 'Sango Kaku'): vase-shaped maple with bright green leaves in spring and summer, turning gold in fall, and coral-red bark in winter. 2/ **Sugar Tip rose of Sharon** (*Hibiscus syriacus* 'America Irene Scott'): variegated rose of Sharon with moonlight-yellow leaf margins and ruffled lavender flowers. 3/ **'Black Diamond' crape myrtle** (*Lagerstroemia indica* 'Black Diamond'): upright crape myrtle with reddish black leaves and flowers that range from white to fuchsia to red in the Black Diamond series. 4/ **Texas mountain laurel** (*Sophora secundiflora*): native tree with glossy evergreen leaves and dangling clusters of sweetly scented purple flowers in spring. 5/ **Liberty holly** (*Ilex* × 'Conty'): pyramidal evergreen with dark green serrated leaves and clusters of red berries in winter. 6/ **Texas redbud** (*Cercis canadensis* var. *texensis*): pink-flowering native tree with heart-shaped, semi-glossy leaves.

EAST
TEXAS

THE PLACE

East Texas is a place of trees and water. Ranks of fringe-needled pines reaching for the sky above a leafy understory. Placid lakes and cypress-columned swamps hung with curtains of Spanish moss, alive with egrets, fish, and alligators. Slow-moving bayous meandering through coastal prairie, draining toward the Gulf.

CLIMATE

Humid subtropical. Summers are long, hot, and humid, and winters are mild, although hard freezes can be expected inland, away from the coast. Rainfall occurs throughout the year, with an annual average of between 40 and 59 inches.

CHALLENGES AHEAD

Summers are growing hotter and longer, and droughts are expected to intensify. Winters will be warmer overall but may bring more extreme cold snaps. Rainfall may remain at similar levels but fall with increased intensity, leading to more runoff and flooding. Tropical storms and hurricanes are expected to grow stronger, thanks to the warming Gulf, increasing the risk of flooding, storm surges, and wind damage.

TAKE ACTION

☐ Install gutters and cisterns to collect and store rainwater.

☐ Install drip irrigation, which is less wasteful and more targeted than overhead sprinklers. Drip is sometimes exempt from municipal watering restrictions because of its efficiency.

☐ Choose native plants, which evolved to survive the weather extremes of their native range, and well-adapted nonnatives that can tolerate record highs and lows, not just average temps.

☐ Add rain gardens to manage runoff.

☐ Remove paving where possible, and plant coastal prairie gardens to soak up heavy rains.

☐ Reduce lawn and replace with groundcovers, low-growing grasses or sedges, and prostrate shrubs.

☐ Create shade by planting trees on the southwest and southeast sides of the garden and by building pergolas or installing shade sails over patios.

INTO THE HEIGHTS

"I DREAM IN FLIGHT," says Mark McKinnon. "I dream as if I can fly. I'm not a bird. I'm not an insect. I'm not something other than who I am. But in my dreams, I fly." During his waking hours, any time that Mark craves the exhilaration of soaring height, he climbs ladder-like stairs to the top of a wooden observation tower in his backyard. From this three-story perch, Mark enjoys a bird's-eye view across the rooftops of his Houston neighborhood toward downtown's high-rises. "It's a place for me to get up and away," he says.

The tower, an architectural folly of Mark's own design, is just one of the vertical features in his garden. His 116-year-old home occupies a small lot in the close-in Heights neighborhood, veiled by a scrim of surprisingly large trees. Mark planted some of these, but others were here when he bought the place in 1988, including an enormous native sycamore that's listed in a book about significant trees in the City of Houston. For Mark, the steep-gabled, bark-brown house with a tin-roofed back porch, sheltered by so many trees, reminds him of a summer camp cabin—a leafy escape from the city. He leaned into that vibe as he began making his garden. "It's an urban woodland garden because I wanted a lot of shade and privacy," he says, "and I wanted to be enveloped by vegetation. There's a tremendous number of trees and plants to fulfill that desire."

In addition to the giant sycamore, his garden contains a thick-trunked pine, an impressive Montezuma cypress and its bald cypress cousin, a row of graceful river birches, and a hatch-trunked palmetto. Hedges of magnolia and holly add green screening along the fences. Below the trees, a dense understory of native dwarf palmetto, sedge, shade-loving grasses, and woodland perennials like spiderwort, oxalis, and Turk's cap adds more greenery and seasonal color. "I've always been devoted to natives," says Mark, "though not exclusively. But the native plants are much more resilient to our extremes of weather. An English gardener I read about once said, 'Find out what grows well in the garden, and then grow a lot of it.' That makes a lot of sense to me." In the more restrained back garden, a small lawn area consists not of sun-loving turfgrass but horseherb, a native groundcover, which Mark overseeds in winter with ryegrass. "I mow maybe once a month in summer," says Mark. A low concrete trough pond with a trickling fountain and mossy, focal-point container of dwarf elephant ear and maidenhair fern anchors the courtyard-like space, surrounded by porches on three sides.

From a young age growing up in Houston, Mark was intrigued by plants and the emotional responses they evoke. "What drew me into gardening," he says, "is the feeling of going someplace different when you are introduced to a garden." As a young man, he considered becoming

OPPOSITE: A three-story observation tower offers a bird's-eye view of the garden and surrounding neighborhood.

FOLLOWING PAGE: Behind a scrim of tree trunks and green foliage, the house nearly disappears despite its urban location.

an architect, but landscape architecture grabbed him instead. By his twenties, he'd started his own firm, McKinnon Associates. That's also when he bought his home and started making the garden—pretty much instantly. "The garden was more of a priority than any project inside," he says. As he cleaned up the yard, he discovered old Houston pavers buried under soil and leaves. He grubbed them out and used them to delineate garden beds and a gravel parking court in front of the house. "I like that connection, given the vintage of the home," says Mark. Early on, he tried to establish an English-style perennial garden but quickly found it was too much work, and the exotic plants didn't thrive in the shade or in Houston's sultry summers. He changed direction, selecting native shade-loving perennials like Gulf Coast penstemon and inland sea oats to give him the lush look he wanted without all the toil and disappointment. "The natives truly are perennial and resilient and tough as nails," he says. During the rare hard freeze, which Houston has experienced more often in recent years, plants may die to the ground, but they come back in spring. "I don't lose things 100 percent," says Mark. "If plants freeze to the ground, I go, 'OK, I'll be patient.' That dimension of a garden and that sense of time is something I've grown into." One of his oldest, most-prized plants is a sago palm as tall and broad as a beach umbrella. "I bought it around 1985 as a 5-gallon plant and kept it in a container while living in an apartment," says Mark. "When I moved here, I planted it in the garden and cultivated it as an upright, single-trunk specimen. That doesn't just happen. It has survived hurricanes, freezes, and droughts."

Making the garden part of his home has driven most of his design decisions. Mark connected interior rooms to the outdoors by aligning garden views with doors and windows, enlarging his living spaces both visually and physically. Three covered porches provide a generous amount of outdoor living space. His

back porch—originally screened until Mark removed the distracting mesh—spans the entire length of the house. Another porch fronts the two-story guesthouse behind his home that he built for his late mother. An open-sided breezeway with a swinging bench connects those two porches. All enjoy regular use. "I have a variety of places to sit," says Mark. "I can sit on the swing and create a breeze. Or I can prop up my feet in a chaise longue and fall asleep reading a book." He hosts an annual Easter dinner on the expansive back porch. "I can only seat four to six people inside comfortably," he says. "But I had sixteen people last Easter at a very long table on the porch."

From any of the porches, Mark enjoys the sight and sound of his trough water feature. "It's a recirculating fountain," he explains. "The water flows up through the pot with aquatic plants in it, and those plants filter the water. I have water clarity year-round even with fish in the pond." A sunken basin parallel to the trough acts as a retention pond when it rains. "Part of my concept of water conservation," says Mark, "is I don't have gutters anywhere on my structures. That may not work for everybody, but it works for me in the soils and conditions I have and the nature of my rooflines. I let rainwater hit the ground and direct it to this basin. So I'm collecting rainwater and giving it a chance to percolate into the soil. It's a microscale way of managing stormwater."

Thirty-five years have passed since Mark first started gardening here, time enough to see saplings mature into garden sentinels and native perennials weave a green understory that waxes and wanes through the seasons. "There was a time," he says, "when I was anxious to have a certain effect and full realization of my vision. But now I'm willing to let the garden be a little more ephemeral. If something freezes to the ground, I wait for it to come back up. And if it starts growing out of the bounds I originally envisioned, that's OK. I say to myself, 'Look, I have this successful plant! Let it fly.'"

ABOVE: Dwarf palmetto makes a jazz-hands hedge that screens the street.

LEFT: Mark McKinnon calls his garden the Tower Garden, named for the folly he built for getting up and away.

ABOVE: White-trunked river birches in a narrow side yard gracefully screen the house next door. A plow-disc gate fabricated by Austin metal artist Lars Stanley separates the garden from a parking court.

RIGHT: For 40 years, Mark has nurtured his prized sago palm, training it into a single-trunked specimen.

OPPOSITE: Water from the pond is drawn up to filter through a pot of aquatic plants—dwarf elephant ear and maidenhair fern—before spilling back into the pool. The biofiltration keeps the water clear.

BELOW: A soaring bald cypress makes a green canopy in the courtyard garden.

RIGHT: The chartreuse front door stands out against the house's bark-brown siding.

OPPOSITE, CLOCKWISE FROM TOP:
On the breezeway between the main house and the guesthouse, a porch swing and chairs provide a relaxing hangout spot. 'Alphonse Karr' bamboo pruned up along the fence is secured with bamboo poles.

The waxy, lemon-scented flowers of 'Kay Parris' magnolia span 8 to 10 inches.

Spiderwort flowers abundantly in spring, attracting foraging bees, and then goes dormant during the heat of summer.

Plant a Groundcover Instead of Lawn

Mark treasures his trees, but their shade means that turfgrass doesn't thrive. Instead of fighting the shade, he planted a small "lawn" of horseherb (inset), a native shade-loving and drought-tolerant groundcover with tiny yellow flowers that feed butterflies. In winter, to keep the space green, he overseeds with annual ryegrass (seen here in April), which lasts until the heat returns, when the horseherb takes center stage again.

"Horseherb does really well in my garden," says Mark. "It's good during drought, and with the expense and shortage of water in Texas, I think it's going to be around for a while." Horseherb naturally stays low, about 5 inches tall, but it can take occasional mowing. Mark runs the mower over it once a month in summer to keep it tidy.

Other shade-loving groundcovers for low-traffic areas include sedges (try Berkeley, Texas, Leavenworth's, or 'Everillo' sedge), river fern, ajuga, and pigeonberry.

Ancient Flora for East Texas

Some prehistoric plants that flourished millions of years ago still thrive today. Mark grows these "living fossils." **1/ Mediterranean fan palm** (*Chamaerops humilis*): slow-growing, shrubby palm with fan-shaped, evergreen leaves and thorny stems. **2/ Umbrella sedge** (*Cyperus alternifolius*): low-growing, parasol-shaped foliage that thrives in boggy soil. **3/ Sago palm** (*Cycas revoluta*): long, arching branches of comb-toothed leaves, eventually forming a woody trunk. **4/ Loblolly pine** (*Pinus taeda*): fast-growing pine tree with fringy clusters of long needles and a tall, scaly trunk. **5/ Southern magnolia** (*Magnolia grandiflora*): large evergreen tree with leathery, glossy leaves and fragrant creamy flowers in spring and summer. Cultivar 'Kay Parris' is more compact. **6/ Bald cypress** (*Taxodium distichum*): handsome tall tree with a buttressed trunk, "knees" that poke up in wet soil, and feathery leaves that turn orange in fall.

THE FARM
NEXT DOOR

LIKE MANY GARDENS, Amy Sutton's doubles as a time machine. Simply by snapping a green bean from its vine and nibbling its raw, green crispiness, Amy is whisked back to her early years on a Virginia farm with a big vegetable garden that she helped tend. "It tastes like my childhood," she says with a smile. Back then, as her schoolmates dreamed of becoming astronauts or teachers or firefighters, young Amy wanted to be a horticulturist. "I was really into plants," she recalls with a laugh. "I had plants at home and tore articles out of magazines like *Southern Living* and ordered those *Time-Life* series on plants."

Amy's flora obsession gave way to other interests as she grew older, and she ended up becoming a partner at an accounting firm instead of a horticulturist. But always in the back of her mind she held space for her dream garden, where she would grow vegetables and relax in a gazebo among trees and flowers. She and husband Gary Chiles settled in Houston's West University neighborhood, in a house with a small, shady backyard unsuitable for growing vegetables. Then an old bungalow next door went up for sale, seemingly destined for a tear-down and big new house. Amy bought it, razed the house (she had it deconstructed by Habitat for Humanity for its reusable building materials), and hired David Morello Garden Enterprises to design and install the garden she'd wanted for so long. Construction began in spring of 2019, and six months later Amy hosted her first garden party. The following spring, the COVID shutdown meant Amy was home all day. "Once I started working from home," she says, "I was able to enjoy the garden all through the pandemic. Gary and I had lunch in the gazebo every day."

The garden's formal design complements the traditional, two-story brick house and includes symmetrical raised beds, boxwood parterres with roses, and a long axis view that runs from the columned entry gate through the brick planters to a substantial screened gazebo. Where there might have been a tall, light-blocking house squeezed in next door, adding impervious cover, today Amy's park-like garden provides a place to commune with nature, open ground for rainfall absorption, and habitat for lizards, birds, and insects, not to mention a bounty of food and the fun of growing it. Four raised beds, each about 3 by 5 feet, give Amy ample space for her favorite vegetables: corn, green beans, broccoli, and squash. In winter, she grows lettuces for salads. While David Morello's crew maintains the ornamental beds, Amy tends the vegetable garden herself, from sowing and transplanting to weeding to harvesting. After some experimentation, she now takes a break during the hot summer months. Fall through spring, however, the four beds produce far more food than she and Gary can eat, and she gives surplus away to friends.

OPPOSITE: Blue anise sage shows off cobalt flowers with nearly black calyxes above lime-green foliage.

FOLLOWING PAGE: Four brick raised beds in the sunny center of the garden provide space for growing vegetables.

Although the garden is only a few years old, Amy's already seeing the effects of hotter summers and cold snaps in winter and has adjusted her planting routine to adapt. "I put things in a little earlier now," she says. "And I only have one or two beds going in winter."

Surrounding the vegetable beds, an ornamental garden of shrubs, perennials, small trees (mainly redbuds, Eagleston hollies, and a Chinese fringetree), and climbing vines softens the tall walls of the house and screens views of neighboring homes. A birdbath and a drilled-rock fountain entice birds and other creatures, and butterflies and bees find sustenance in colorfully flowering salvias, lantana, and Turk's cap. Amy plants milkweed to feed monarch caterpillars, and she and Gary enjoy searching for their jade-green chrysalises. "It's amazing where you can find them," says Amy. "They climb all the way up the wall to the second story of our house and our neighbor's house. Sometimes they hang from the top of the gazebo." Amy installed rain barrels to collect roof runoff and

fills her watering cans from them to soak her vegetables with pure rainwater. Otherwise, the garden is watered through a combination of efficient drip irrigation and tree bubblers, plus spray heads around the perimeter.

A rectangular, hip-roofed gazebo with screened walls and doors provides an elegant focal point for the garden and helps hide power lines and tall neighboring houses. It also offers a sheltered and mosquito-proof spot from which to enjoy the garden. Inside, a fan and lighting extend its useability. "Most days I eat lunch in the gazebo, unless it's really cold," Amy says. The notoriously hot and muggy Houston summer doesn't always keep her indoors either. "Even in the low 90s I'll still go out there. It has a fan and is comfortable." On weekends she lounges in the gazebo for hours, catching up on her reading. She also likes that she can observe neighborhood comings and goings—kids playing, the postal worker walking by—from her hideaway. The privacy it affords is especially welcome because the garden can be seen from the street and neighboring houses. That was by design. Amy wanted the garden to be a place of beauty that her neighbors could enjoy, not hidden away behind a solid fence. The open metal fence that she chose is a generous gesture, offering views of the garden to parents and kids walking by, joggers, and dog walkers. "We're sharing with everyone," Amy says. "It's sort of like a community garden." She adds with a laugh, "Don't just walk in. But you're welcome to look!"

From the Virginia farm of her childhood to her urban Houston neighborhood today, Amy has come full circle, once again growing her own food, paying attention to green things, and delighting in their beauty or flavor. Farmer Amy, she jokingly calls herself. The young girl fascinated by plants and envisioning a future with them brought her dream garden to life.

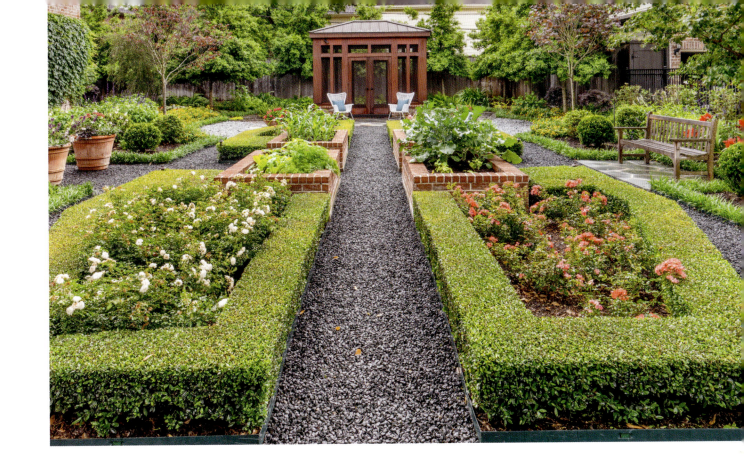

ABOVE: The garden's main axis passes through boxwood parterres with roses and raised vegetable beds to a screened gazebo.

LEFT: When the house next door came up for sale, Amy Sutton saw an opportunity to create the garden she'd long dreamed about.

OPPOSITE: Different types of stone—flagstone, beach pebbles, and gravel, all in shades of gray—add texture to the garden's paving. Feathery foxtail fern leads the eye to a hot-pink pelargonium in a terracotta bowl planter.

ABOVE: Broccoli is one of Amy's favorite cool-season vegetables.

RIGHT: The metal fence offers views of the garden to passersby. Owl finials represent the mascot of Rice University, Amy and Gary's alma mater.

OPPOSITE: The graceful lavender flowers of society garlic are a pollinator favorite.

ABOVE: A small patio at the back door offers another sitting area. Virginia creeper greens the brick wall until fall, when leaves turn scarlet and blue berries, beloved by birds, ripen.

OPPOSITE, CLOCKWISE FROM TOP LEFT: Pots of pentas, sweet potato vine, gaura, and angelonia add seasonal color. A rain barrel under a downspout stores rainwater that Amy uses for her vegetables.

Fragrant mandevillea vine twines up the fence.

A drilled-rock fountain's gentle splash adds the sound of water and attracts birds.

Annual zinnias feed butterflies and make pretty cut flowers for vases.

Plant a Garden that Feeds People *and* Pollinators

When planting a garden to put fresh food on your table, make space for pollinator food too. That is, include flowering plants nearby that attract bees and other insects by providing nectar and pollen. Visiting bees will return the favor by pollinating crops like peppers, squash, cucumbers, and fruit trees, increasing their yield. It's a win-win arrangement.

Pollinators are in decline across Texas. Every patch of salvia, zinnia, society garlic, milkweed, and lantana—just a few of the pollinator-friendly plants that Amy grows—helps them out, and we need them more than we know.

Amy's Favorite Spring Vegetables

1/ 'True Gold' sweet corn: a heavy feeder that needs a lot of organic fertilizer, which should be added to the soil two weeks before planting. Corn is wind pollinated, explains Amy, so "you need to plant enough of one variety, all at the same time, so that they'll tassel at the same time" and pollinate the silks to form ears of corn. Planting in a block formation, rather than rows, helps ensure pollination, as does gently shaking the stalks to release pollen from the tassels. Amy plants corn in early March and harvests in late May. "It's not 'knee high by the Fourth of July,' as the saying goes," she notes. "In Houston, it's long been harvested by then."

2/ Broccoli: spring-planted broccoli must be grown from transplants, not seed, to beat the heat in Houston, and it needs regular water. Amy plants in early February and begins harvesting in late March. "After cutting a head of broccoli— or sometimes if a big head never forms—florets continue to grow, which are nice for salads," says Amy.

3/ 'Contender' bush green beans: "One of my most satisfying crops, with great spring and fall harvests," says Amy. In Houston, which is USDA Plant Hardiness Zone 9b, plant in early March and again in early April. Beans will be ready to pick at the beginning of May and into June.

DRAWING ON NATURE

WHENEVER ARTIST Dixie Friend Gay seeks inspiration, she need only lie flat on her stomach and examine her garden from a bug's-eye view. At least, that's how her glass mosaic mural "Wild Wonderland" began, one of many large-scale artworks Dixie has made for parks, airports, universities, and other public spaces across Texas and the United States. A prolific creator, Dixie expresses herself through mosaic, sculpture, painting, and drawing, but also through the wildlife-welcoming garden surrounding her Houston home. The garden is, she finds, an ever-changing canvas, alive with lizards, bees, butterflies, wasps, and birds, with seedlings that reach for the light and flowers unfurling every month of the year. What she observes here—leaves and petals, water and sunlight, cycles of life and death—flows through her imagination and is expressed in her nature-centric work. "There's no separation between my garden and my art," Dixie says. "It's all one. Everything I do is art, garden, art."

Dixie's home and studio sit on a large lot—⅔ of an acre—in the close-to-downtown Heights neighborhood. Along the back, a spring-fed creek flows into White Oak Bayou, one of the slow-moving waterways that drain the tortilla-flat, flood-prone city. The creek attracts wildlife, including herons that roost in the trees and occasionally nab a goldfish from Dixie's pond. On cold winter mornings, fog rises from the water like steam, and during Houston's sauna-like summer, creek-chilled air cools the adjacent garden.

"It's about 10 degrees cooler here," Dixie says. "I can really tell a difference."

On occasion, though, during tropical storms, the creek goes rogue, swelling over its banks and submerging the garden—or worse. Twice, floodwaters invaded Dixie's home, most recently in 2017, when Hurricane Harvey pushed in over a foot of water. Afterward, Dixie had her house and studio demolished and rebuilt at an elevation of 9 feet. Even her saltwater swimming pool and a secondary studio are elevated several feet. The garden endures, minus the plants that didn't survive the floods, and it's a sunnier space than it once was. "Being along the creek means that sometimes the garden is essentially part of the creek," says Dixie, "and this changes the composition of the soil. It also makes changes I did not plan to the tree canopy and the smaller trees and shrubs in the understory. We were going for a partially shaded garden, but sometimes nature has other plans. A garden requires resilience and a sense of humor."

Dixie knows that climate change will bring more flooding to Houston in the years ahead, but she also believes in the power of individual action, including in landscaping decisions, to make a difference. "Like so many places in Coastal Texas and all over the world now, the water is coming for us," Dixie says.

OPPOSITE: A glass mosaic birdbath repeats the cobalt hue of blue anise sage's flowers.

FOLLOWING PAGE: A faun ornament echoes the color and curved form of lizard's tail flowers. Chunks of blue glass laid among the rocks make a water-like ribbon of color.

"I think everybody should capture the water coming off their house and driveway and not let it just rush out into the ditches, into the streets, into the creeks. If we all were responsible for the water on our property and allowed it to release slowly, we wouldn't have a flooding issue." To that end, Dixie installed gutters and put in two 1000-gallon cisterns to capture roof runoff, and she built terraces in her garden near the creekbank to slow erosion and allow rainwater to soak into the soil.

Devoting more of the garden to green space and reducing impervious cover helps prevent flooding too. Dixie removed a big chunk of paving from her back garden and enlarged the central planting bed. Forgoing lawn in favor of deep-rooted native and adapted plants helps the garden soak up water like a sponge when it rains. Such plants often prove tenacious during drought too. Her daughter Persephone Hagen, manager of a local nursery, helps Dixie choose plants and solve gardening problems that crop up. "Sephie has a memory like a steel trap for the year we bought a plant, the Latin name, the problems with it," says Dixie. Both women take special delight in plants that attract pollinators, and Persephone watches over a collection of lesser-known native plants from the Gulf Coast prairies with pride. Above all, plant diversity allows for resilience in the face of weather extremes. "Some plants are going to do better when we have a drought," says Dixie. "Others will survive a flood. Others can take a freeze and die to the roots and recover."

Dixie grew up in western Oklahoma on a cattle ranch 30 miles from the nearest town. As a child, she and her siblings had ranch chores, which taught her the difficulties of wresting a living from the land. "We gardened and put out a hundred tomato plants," she says. "We milked our own cows and churned our own butter. We sold eggs. We had a cow-and-calf operation. It was hard work. It was not South Fork." As soon as she could, she left Oklahoma with the intention of

never doing ranch work again. She made her way to New York City, finding success as an artist. Even in that urban environment, though, her art was all about the natural world, reflecting her conservation ethos and belief in oneness with nature.

A move to Houston was meant to be temporary when Dixie relocated with her then-husband and a new baby, but she fell in love with the city. The warm welcome from Houston's art community and the warm climate both appealed to her. They bought the Heights property along the creek 35 years ago, after Dixie found it in foreclosure. "The lot was overgrown with poison ivy, and there was a collapsing building," she remembers. "It took us a few years to clean it up and understand what kind of garden belonged on the site." After a few early missteps—she rues planting a lawn and nonnative groundcovers like liriope and Asian jasmine—the back garden evolved into a naturalistic, meadow-like space with a pond for wildlife. In front, a path curves through a relaxed garden with palms, cycads, and pines adding vertical punctuation.

Dixie's parrot, Baby, often accompanies her in the garden, perching in a tree as Dixie pokes about, looking for new flowers or insect cocoons or changing leaves. Dixie calls her urban oasis Gratitude Garden. "I'm grateful for every time the sun rises, filtering through the trees," she says. "I'm grateful that I can go out my door and not feel like I'm in the city." Working the soil and tending plants makes her feel grounded, and she celebrates each turn of the seasons. "Gardens are about beginnings, of new buds and seedlings," says Dixie. "Gardens are also about endings—clearing dead branches after a drought or a freeze, or finding a peaceful place to bury a songbird. I think my garden is really beautiful right after a freeze, the way plants slump and still have a bit of green but also amber. The plants are just so beautiful. And I know they're going to come back."

ABOVE: The elevated house and art studio overlook the meadow-like back garden, pond, and swimming pool.

LEFT: Dixie Friend Gay finds artistic inspiration in her garden. Persephone Hagen, her daughter, helps with planting advice and troubleshooting.

ABOVE: A bee zooms toward a Louisiana iris.

ABOVE RIGHT: An anole flashes its dewlap in a courting or territorial display.

RIGHT: Baby the parrot keeps Dixie company in the garden.

OPPOSITE: Magenta blossoms of a tropical water lily add jewel-bright color to the pond.

ABOVE: Dixie tiled her swimming pool with a glass-and-porcelain mosaic in a watery design.

RIGHT: The showy flowers of a pink-and-white crinum, rescued from a nearby property where a house was being torn down, open in April.

OPPOSITE, CLOCKWISE FROM TOP LEFT: Yellow cestrum's tubular flowers are sweetly fragrant and attract hummingbirds and pollinators.

Translucent seedpods catch the light on a redbud tree that seeded itself years ago in Dixie's garden.

In the front garden, a palm and sago palm sprout new fronds after an unusually cold winter. Pink and yellow four o'clocks pump out tubular flowers.

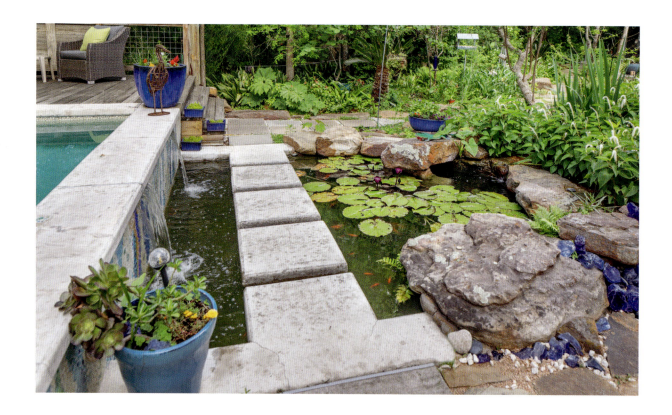

Make a Bog Filter Pond

A garden pond of any size offers the pleasant sight and sound of water, the enjoyment of watching fish and wildlife like birds and dragonflies, and the beauty of waterlilies and other wetland plants. But keeping the water clear and free of algae is a common maintenance problem, one that chemical algaecide or UV-light treatment only temporarily fixes.

A bog filter, on the other hand, cleans pond water naturally and keeps it clear. It works like this: a pump draws water up out of the pond through perforated PVC pipe, which runs through a separate bog filled with pebbles, water, and living bog plants. Beneficial bacteria on the pebbles converts organic waste in the water into plant food, which the bog plants absorb as the water flows up through their roots. After filtering through the bog, water spills back into the pond, clean and clear.

The surface area of the bog should be about ¼ of the size of the main pond, and shallow, no deeper than 12 inches. Place it alongside the main pond or above it, as in Dixie's garden. Her bog filter sits a little higher than her lily pond, separated by large rocks and lush with white-flowering lizard's tail and Louisiana iris. For small ponds, a shallow container that's elevated above and behind the pond can work well. Search online for how-to instructions, along with recommended plants for your bog filter.

Dixie's Bog Filter Plants

1/ 'Full Eclipse' Louisiana iris (*Iris* 'Full Eclipse'): velvety purple flowers and upright, sword-like leaves distinguish this water-loving iris.

2/ Lizard's tail (*Saururus cernuus*): native marsh plant with curling, fluffy white flowers and heart-shaped leaves.

3/ Pond water trickles through the pebbles and plants of the bog filter, which cleans the water naturally, before spilling back into the pond.

CELEBRATING THE EPHEMERAL

WHEN HORTICULTURE PROFESSOR Dr. Jared Barnes isn't busy teaching his students at Stephen F. Austin State University in Nacogdoches, or overseeing the student botanic garden on campus, or interviewing a fascinating figure in the world of horticulture for *The Plantastic Podcast*, you might find him in a field near a construction-coming-soon sign, shovel in hand, digging up native plants like dwarf wild indigo before development plows them under. "I hope to get some of those natives into cultivation," says Jared of his lesser-known rescues. "My own garden is not purely native, but I do love to focus on them because they offer so much in our landscapes. Gardens are a place where we need to create ecosystems to share with other creatures and organisms around us."

Jared grew up in rural Tennessee and started gardening as a youngster, poking seeds into the earth before he'd even hit grade school. As an adult, after a stint as a patio gardener—he tended 100 containers at one point—he longed for a place of his own where he could really let loose. In 2017, he and wife Karen purchased a log house on 2½ acres on the outskirts of Nacogdoches. The gently sloping property was mostly turfgrass with a few mature trees. Jared saw a blank canvas and welcome solitude. "It's so nice to be in a place where you can go out at night and lie on the driveway and see all the constellations," he says. "The other night I heard a chuck-will's-widow across the road."

Jared let the grass grow long the first year, watching to see what came up in it. He discovered sedges, common selfheal, and ladies' tresses orchids in the turfgrass and encouraged them to spread. As he started planting, he aimed for a naturalistic style inspired by Dutch designer Piet Oudolf, adding as many species as he could find that would thrive in the highly acidic soil. Jared believes that a diversity of plants helps the garden survive tough times. "Instead of just rose bushes and crape myrtles around my house," he says, "I now have a mix of about 30 different species. When you go that route, even if 10 percent of them fail, that's only three out of 30. That means I've got 27 other species that can potentially do something in that growing season. To me, that's a resilient approach to gardening."

By growing plants native to East Texas, especially those that entice pollinators, Jared sees his garden as a curated version of the wild. He encourages plants to knit together by spacing them closely, leaving little bare soil for weeds to get a foothold or for runoff to create a problem. He uses groundcovers like sedge and self-sowers like sandyland bluebonnets, baby blue eyes, and selfheal to further reduce weed pressure and necessitate less mulching. "I'm trying to create a planting that is able to sustain itself," he says.

OPPOSITE: Indian plantain grows swiftly in early spring, providing welcome height and interesting foliage.

FOLLOWING PAGE: A bumblebee collects pollen from a nodding penstemon flower, against a backdrop of pink downy phlox.

His garden is less than five years old but already provides a vibrant habitat for beneficial and entertaining wildlife. He and Karen especially enjoy watching monarchs visit their garden, and they plant milkweed to feed the caterpillars. "Having plantings that can support insects, pollinators, birds, bees, butterflies, all these things—you know, we're facing a crisis, and their numbers are plummeting," says Jared. "We've got to have places for them to live and survive."

Jared added a large vegetable garden at the back of the property and enjoys growing tomatoes, Swiss chard, garden peas, broccoli, sweet potatoes, peppers, and pumpkins. When deer and rabbits began nibbling and armadillos started uprooting, he built a double fence around the vegetable plots, which proved effective. The first fence keeps out the smaller animals, and a second fence built close inside the first one deters deer from leaping in. Other challenges don't have an easy fix. Winter Storm Uri in 2021 brought a weeklong deep freeze, around 8 inches of snow, and six days without power. "I thought after moving to Texas I was never going to see a good snowfall again," Jared says with a laugh. "We have more extremes now. The hottest temperature I've experienced has been in Texas, and the coldest temperature I've experienced has been in Texas."

Jared's training as a horticulturist gives him unique insights into the effects of more extreme weather events on Texas gardens. With hotter, longer summers, he says, plants are slower to go dormant in the fall, and they wake up earlier in the spring. That makes them more vulnerable to an early or late freeze. He also thinks extreme cold snaps may lead East Texas gardeners to rely less on evergreen shrubs, which historically have kept Southern gardens green year-round. "This is hypothetical," he says, "but if broadleaf evergreens are getting killed to the ground every few years because of freak cold, that's something we'll have to change." Jared remains bullish on native plants and would like to see more East Texas gardeners growing them. "I have faith that our natives will adapt," he says. "But if we start to see struggles with them, we can always pull natives from another ecosystem here in Texas. And I don't mind using some well-adapted exotics that don't have a negative impact on our ecosystem."

In July 2023, Jared and Karen welcomed a baby daughter, Magnolia May. Along with the joys of new parenthood, they relish the fleeting, seasonal changes they observe in their garden, which they've dubbed Ephemera Farm. "We love to celebrate small moments of wonder," says Jared, "like monarchs laying eggs on milkweed in spring. And in summer, that first sun-ripened tomato you pick and put on a delicious turkey-and-mayonnaise sandwich. And then autumn comes, and you've got that first good rain that primes the fall vegetable garden, and pollinators going crazy on asters. And in winter, watching birds flit from seedhead to seedhead. Every moment is small and seems insignificant, but I see the preciousness in ordinary things."

ABOVE: Downy phlox edges a collection of potted annuals and bulbs along the front porch.

LEFT: On their rural property with a log cabin home, Jared and Karen Barnes try to emulate nature in the garden and celebrate the wildness of East Texas.

OPPOSITE: Jared uses sectioned tree trunks as garden edging, a nod to the home's log construction.

ABOVE: 'Powderblue' blueberry has multi-season interest with white, bell-shaped flowers, pink berries ripening to light blue, and crimson leaves in fall.

RIGHT: Potted succulents and a pail-planted dusty miller on the front porch pair with vintage bricks, an old watering can, and a stump for down-home charm.

OPPOSITE: Yellow wild indigo and Gulf Coast penstemon make a pollinator banquet along the vegetable garden fence.

LEFT: A fresh-picked bouquet dresses up a pair of garden chairs near the vegetable garden.

BELOW: Downy phlox makes a pink haze in the early spring garden.

OPPOSITE, CLOCKWISE FROM TOP: The meadowy garden contains a diversity of plants native to East Texas and is intended to be shared with wildlife. As a fun accent, Jared and Karen hang potted succulents on their porch posts, bringing the garden right up to the front door.

Scarlet penstemon makes a siren song for hummingbirds.

A black swallowtail butterfly nectars on phlox.

Cater a Pollinator Buffet

We depend on insects like bees, flies, wasps, beetles, moths, and butterflies more than we may realize. They pollinate many human and livestock food crops and around 75 percent of all flowering plant species on earth. Without them, these plants could not make seed and reproduce naturally. According to the U.S. Fish and Wildlife Service, many species of bees and other pollinators are disappearing due to habitat loss, disease, and pesticide use. But providing habitat in our home gardens can help. Pollinator insects need five things.

» **FLOWERING PLANTS** Pollinators are drawn to flowers for pollen and/or nectar, which they use for food for themselves or their larvae. Different species of insects need different types of flowers suited to their tongue length, so plant as many kinds as you have room for. Diversity is good. If you can, add lesser-known native plants to the mix, as Jared does, to attract insects that rely on those.

» **LARVAL HOST PLANTS** Pollinating insects look for particular plants on which to lay their eggs because once they hatch, the larvae need those plants for food. Monarch butterflies are best known for this. They lay eggs on milkweed, which is the only plant monarch caterpillars can eat. When you plant a host plant, expect that caterpillars will eat it to a nub. That means you're feeding the next generation of butterflies and moths.

» **WATER** Provide a water source for thirsty pollinators. A shallow dish of water, a pond with a flat rock at the surface, and even a gravelly puddle offer safe options for insects to get a drink.

» **SHELTER** Like all creatures, pollinators need safe places to rest and nest. Some species nest in the ground or in piles of debris, so allow for a patch of undisturbed bare soil and a small pile of sticks. Others overwinter in the pithy stems of plants or among leaves, so resist tidying the garden too neatly in fall. Allow freeze-browned plants to stand through winter, and cut them back just before new growth begins. You can also bundle short pieces of bamboo or drill holes partway in a block of wood to make a "bee hotel."

» **AVOID PESTICIDES** To protect pollinators that visit your garden, be tolerant of insect damage on plants, and avoid spraying for bugs, including mosquito spraying. If you must treat, use on a non-windy day to avoid drift, apply before dawn or near sunset, when pollinators are less likely to be actively foraging, and do not apply to flowering plants.

Native Pollinator Plants for East Texas

1/ **Yellow wild indigo** (*Baptisia sphaerocarpa*): rounded blue-green leaves with spires of butter-yellow flowers in spring and rattling seedpods in late summer. 2/ **Gulf Coast penstemon** (*Penstemon tenuis*): lavender, bell-shaped flowers on upright stems above lance-shaped leaves. 3/ **Willowleaf aster** (*Symphyotrichum praealtum*): pale lavender flowers with yellow centers appear in autumn, attracting butterflies and bees. 4/ **Prairie larkspur** (*Delphinium carolinianum*): short-lived perennial with azure flowers on tall stems in spring and summer. 5/ **Indian plantain** (*Arnoglossum plantagineum*): rubbery leaves and pinstriped, red-and-green stems, which hold clusters of white flowers in spring. 6/ **Oldplainsman** (*Hymenopappus artemisiifolius*): biennial with branching white flowers that blush pink in spring, attracting butterflies. 7/ **'Grape Sensation' Winkler's blanketflower** (*Gaillardia aestivalis* var. *winkleri* 'Grape Sensation'): plentiful purple flowers spring through fall on this cultivar of a rare East Texas native perennial. 8/ **Butterfly milkweed** (*Asclepias tuberosa*): showy orange flower clusters from spring through fall attract butterflies, and it's a larval host plant for monarchs. 9/ **Swamp sunflower** (*Helianthus angustifolius*): tall branching stalks with abundant yellow flowers from late summer through fall.

THE SCULPTED GARDEN

AN ARRANGEMENT OF potted cacti and succulents on the porch steps of Don Bayer and Greg Lofgren's bungalow invites visitors to slow down and look. Is this rain-blessed Houston or someplace farther west? A sword-leaved agave pokes above a clipped hedge, adding to the South-meets-Southwest frisson. In back, a few agaves accent a gravel patio where boxwood globes make an undulating, cloud-like formation. Horizontal planks of boxwood and a stacked-stone wall bisect the contemporary space.

These exquisitely composed, almost sculptural vignettes with a southwestern edge reflect the artistic talents of both Don and Greg and their fondness for the modern yet lushly planted courtyard gardens at Hotel San José in Austin, 165 miles to the west. "We like the feel of the San José," says Greg. "That was really the impetus for our garden." The couple is also inspired by Japanese gardens and teahouses, particularly their use of rock and arrangements of containers and topiary. For Greg, a graphic designer and painter, and Don, a sculptor, every aspect of their Museum District home and garden is an opportunity to express their creativity. "For me, creative endeavors are all the same," says Greg, "whether you're cooking or doing interiors or making outdoor rooms. If you're creative, it's all connected. It overlaps in every part of your life." Artful moments abound in their garden: a trophy wall of antler-esque staghorn ferns; a delicate tendril of fig ivy tracing its way across red brick; a row of pink and gray stones atop a wall;

a collection of old gardening tools precisely arrayed on a fence.

Don and Greg started making their garden about 25 years ago, dividing it into outdoor rooms to visually expand their interiors and make their 1400-square-foot bungalow live larger. "We've both learned over the years," says Greg, "that it's not significant square footage that makes a house livable or wonderful. It's how we use our spaces. A small house can feel twice its size with a thoughtful garden simply because there are as many usable spaces outside as inside." About ten years in, they hired landscape architect Mark McKinnon to help them organize the garden with pathways and a new gated entrance. In back, a hall-like arbor was built to arch high over a teak table and chairs. In spring, Rangoon creeper vines return from their winter cut-back to climb the pillars, and by summer their dangling flower clusters—which emerge white and then turn pink and wine-red, with all three colors showing at once—scent the patio. "That's my favorite plant in the yard," says Don. "In summer it is so beautiful, and it blooms all the time and smells wonderful."

The couple asked Mark to redesign the

OPPOSITE: The backyard courtyard garden is defined by evergreen hedges, low walls, and curated arrangements of potted plants and art objects.

FOLLOWING PAGE: An arched arbor, cloaked by Rangoon creeper come summer, shelters a teak dining table in the back garden. Wide steps along the house provide access from multiple doors, allowing the home and garden to function as one.

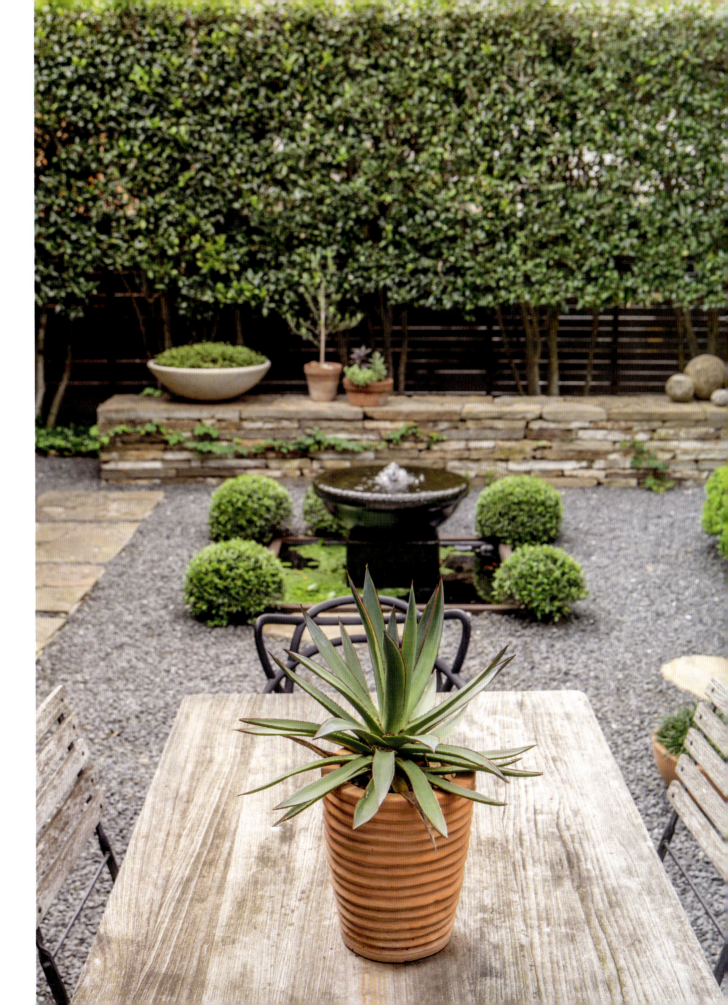

rear garden after Don tired of maintaining a large koi pond that once dominated the space. Mark pulled out the pond and a flagstone patio and reused the stone in a long, stacked wall that provides bench seating and display space for Greg's pots. Dark gray gravel was laid throughout for rainwater-permeable paving. A new, smaller fishpond with a fountain provides the sight and sound of water with less maintenance. Mark intentionally left open space for his clients to play around with. "Mark understands that Donny and I enjoy doing things," says Greg. "I'm notorious for rearranging things, inside and out. Around the pecan tree, Mark said, 'Here's an empty space for moving things around.' The stone bench, that's the same thing. We've had it full of plants. And then I take all the plants off. I look at the garden as an outdoor living space, so it's like moving furniture. I'm constantly arranging."

Recently, to create more privacy, the couple added a trellis screen along the side of the house, which Don greened up with his collection of staghorn ferns, most of them divided from a single plant he purchased back in 1974. The leafy, branching air plants, mounted on wooden boards, make a striking living screen that can be enjoyed through the dining room window and from the front porch, where Don, Greg, and Matty, their whippet, spend much of their time. Even when they're indoors, the garden remains a key part of their home. "What you want to do is bring the garden inside the house," says Don, by composing views framed by windows and doorways.

Some recent changes to their garden have been made not by choice but by Mother Nature. For years, evergreen star jasmine swathed the wire fence around the front yard, providing privacy. But extreme freezes killed it two years in a row, and Don and Greg are debating whether to replace it again. Boxwood blight arrived and ran like wildfire through a treasured hedge. They replaced that hedge with dwarf yaupon, a native evergreen that can be shaped, but are hoping to keep their remaining boxwood. "I love clipping it," says Greg. "It's meditative." Don agrees that tending the garden brings them a lot of joy. "I really enjoy working with those staghorn ferns," he says. Whether by choice or necessity, a garden is always changing. As artists, Don and Greg delight in sculpting their garden, continually reshaping it into its new, best version of itself.

ABOVE: Potted boxwood balls echo sculptural orbs on the stone wall.

LEFT: Greg Lofgren and Don Bayer, both artists, see the garden as an opportunity to express themselves creatively through plant collections and artistic arrangements.

OPPOSITE: A spiny agave makes a sculptural focal point against a leafy wall of Virginia creeper.

ABOVE: Golden-stemmed 'Alphonse Karr' bamboo softens a side fence and screens the house next door.

RIGHT: A collection of potted cacti and succulents greets visitors near the front door.

OPPOSITE: A potted agave, softened by trailing nasturtium, shows off spiky foliage against the home's red brick and midnight blue doors.

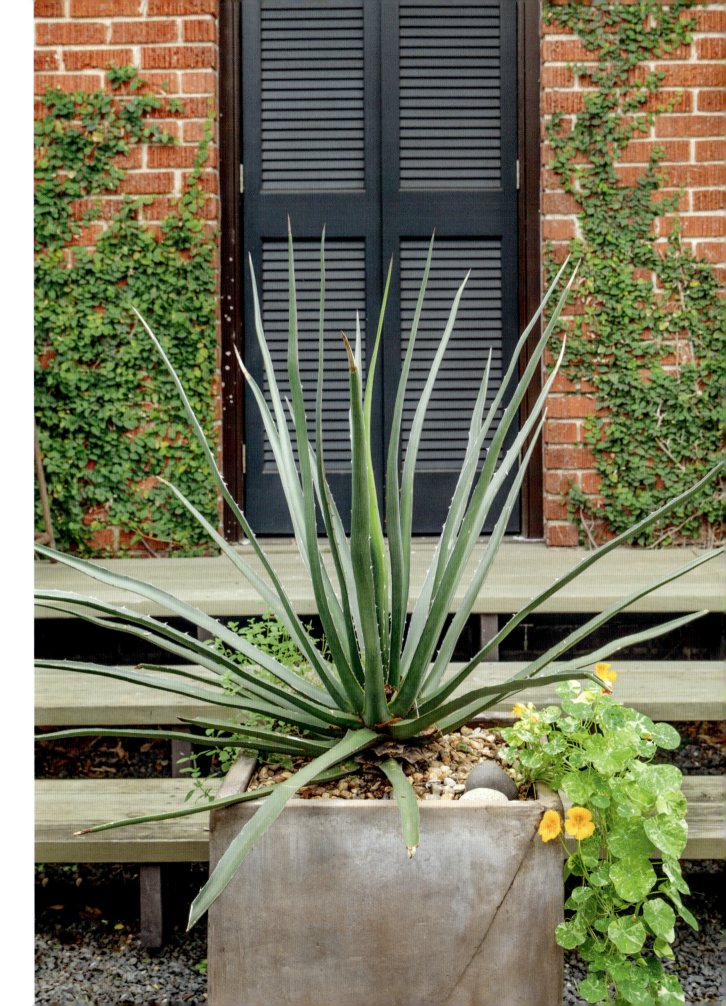

ABOVE: Ghost plant in a faux bois pot makes a textural, gray focal point against a slatted screen, where a few of Don's staghorn ferns and garden tools are neatly displayed.

LEFT: Fragrant Rangoon creeper is Don's favorite plant.

OPPOSITE, CLOCKWISE FROM TOP:
A fountain splashes into a small fishpond in the gravel courtyard. Greg enjoys arranging potted plants and art objects on the stone wall.

Don's collection of staghorn ferns hangs on a slatted screen that gives privacy to the front porch.

Don and Greg spend a lot of time on their deep front porch. They put in a small artificial lawn for their pup, Matty, after their turf got shaded out by trees.

LEFT: Fig ivy clings to the red brick of the house.

BELOW LEFT: Greg cradles Matty the whippet.

BELOW: A barbed-wire sphere under a sinuous live oak limb adorns the side garden path.

ABOVE: Cement orbs and a 25-year-old ficus bonsai are displayed on the stone wall—until Greg gets an urge to rearrange.

LEFT: Neatly stacked terracotta pots make a pretty vignette in the potting area.

Bring Home a Place You Love

Sometimes a place speaks to us and makes us long to bring that feeling home. Maybe it's a pergola-shaded bench at a local park, a favorite bistro's patio garden, or a beautiful garden visited on tour. For Don and Greg, the lush garden courtyards of Hotel San José, a boutique hotel in Austin, inspired them to translate its ambience into their own garden. Here's how they brought inspiration home.

» **ADAPT HARDSCAPING MATERIALS** Fencing at the hotel consists of horizontal 2-inch-by-2-inch cedar slats with see-through spacing. Greg and Don built two such screens—one to hide their potting area and another to display Don's staghorn ferns—although they altered the scale to suit their needs. They also liked the hotel's gravel paving but chose a different type and color that worked better with their house.

» **CHOOSE SIMILAR PLANTS** Potted cacti and succulents caught their eye at the hotel, so they potted up a collection of their own. Likewise, low boxwood hedges and bamboo screening at the hotel inspired the couple to add clipped boxwood and pruned-up bamboo at home.

» **EMULATE A FOCAL POINT** The couple's bubbling water feature outlined with rusty metal edging was gleaned from the hotel's landscaping, says Greg. Decorative fountains, lighting, containers, and garden art are all ripe for translating into your own garden.

Remember, it's the mood that a place evokes, rather than any particular object, that gives it power in our imaginations. Recreate the mood, and you've brought that place home.

Evergreen Shrubs for Shaping in East Texas

1/ **Boxwood** (*Buxus microphylla*) at left and **dwarf yaupon holly** (*Ilex vomitoria* 'Nana') at right: boxwood is a small-leaved evergreen easily clipped into globes and hedges, but it's susceptible to boxwood blight. Choose cultivars with blight resistance like 'Winter Gem' and 'Wintergreen'. Or opt for native dwarf yaupon. It features a naturally rounded shape and bright green new growth that matures to dark green.

2/ **Burford holly** (*Ilex cornuta* 'Burfordii'): bushy shrub with pointy, glossy, dark green leaves and red berries in winter.

3/ **Bright 'N Tight Carolina cherry laurel** (*Prunus caroliniana* 'Monus'): upright shrub with shiny, pointy leaves and fragrant white flowers in spring.

RESOURCES

NATIVE TEXAS SEED SUPPLIERS

Bamert Seed Company
www.bamertseed.com

Douglass King Seeds
www.dkseeds.com

Native American Seed
www.seedsource.com

Wildseed Farms
www.wildseedfarms.com

PLANT DATABASES

Grow Green plant list
www.austintexas.gov/department/grow-green/plant-guide

Native Plant Society of Texas database
www.npsot.org/resources/native-plants/
native-plants-database

**Native Plants of North America database,
Lady Bird Johnson Wildflower Center**
www.wildflower.org/plants-main

Texas SmartScape plant search
www.txsmartscape.com/plant-search

TELEVISION

Central Texas Gardener
produced by Austin PBS, KLRU-TV
www.centraltexasgardener.org

BOTANICAL GARDENS, PARKS, AND PRESERVES

Chihuahuan Desert Nature Center and Botanical Gardens,
Fort Davis

Dallas Arboretum and Botanical Garden

Fort Worth Botanic Garden

Houston Botanic Garden

The John Fairey Garden, Hempstead

Kinder Land Bridge and Prairie, Houston

Lady Bird Johnson Wildflower Center, Austin

Laura W. Bush Native Texas Park, Dallas

Quinta Mazatlan, McAllen

San Antonio Botanical Garden

Selah, Bamberger Ranch Preserve, Johnson City

Shangri La Botanical Gardens and Nature Center, Orange

Tandy Hills Natural Area, Fort Worth

Tobin Land Bridge, San Antonio

Zilker Botanical Garden, Austin

BOOKS

American Roots: Lessons and Inspiration from the Designers Reimagining Our Home Gardens (2022) by Nick McCullough, Allison McCullough, and Teresa Woodard

How to Grow Native Plants of Texas and the Southwest, revised and updated edition (2001) by Jill Nokes

Lawn Gone! Low-Maintenance, Sustainable, Attractive Alternatives for Your Yard (2013) by Pam Penick

Marfa Garden: The Wonders of Dry Desert Plants (2019) by Jim Fissel, Martha Hughes, Jim Martinez, and Mary Lou Saxon

Native Texas Plants: Landscaping Region by Region (2003) by Sally Wasowski and Andy Wasowski

Nature's Best Hope: A New Approach to Conservation That Starts in Your Yard (2020) by Douglas W. Tallamy

Plant-Driven Design: Creating Gardens that Honor Plants, Place, and Spirit (2008) by Scott Ogden and Lauren Springer Ogden

Planting in a Post-Wild World: Designing Plant Communities for Resilient Landscapes (2015) by Thomas Rainer and Claudia West

The Pollinator Victory Garden: Win the War on Pollinator Decline with Ecological Gardening (2020) by Kim Eierman

Texas Getting Started Garden Guide: Grow the Best Flowers, Shrubs, Trees, Vines & Groundcovers (2013) by Mary Irish

Texas Month-by-Month Gardening: What to Do Each Month to Have a Beautiful Garden All Year (2014) by Robert "Skip" Richter

The Texas Native Plant Primer: 225 Plants for an Earth-Friendly Garden (2025) by Andrea DeLong-Amaya and the Lady Bird Johnson Wildflower Center

Under Western Skies: Visionary Gardens from the Rocky Mountains to the Pacific Coast (2021) by Caitlin Atkinson and Jennifer Jewell

The View from Federal Twist: A New Way of Thinking About Gardens, Nature and Ourselves (2021) by James Golden

Visionary: Gardens and Landscapes for Our Future (2024) by Claire Takacs with Giacomo Guzzon

The Water-Saving Garden: How to Grow a Gorgeous Garden with a Lot Less Water (2016) by Pam Penick

Waterwise Plants for Sustainable Gardens: 200 Drought-Tolerant Choices for All Climates (2011) by Lauren Springer Ogden and Scott Ogden

Wildflowers of Texas (2018) by Michael Eason

Annuals 'Ruby Parfait' celosia and
'Ping Pong White' gomphrena flower
riotously in Jared Barnes's garden in
Nacogdoches.

PHOTOGRAPHY CREDITS

All photographs are by Kenny Braun, except for the following:

Jared Barnes, pages 373 (top-right, middle row, bottom row), 391, 394
Meredith Edgley, page 336 (inset)
Pam Penick, pages 28 (top, bottom),
    73 (middle-center, middle-right, bottom row),
    97 (top-middle, top-right, bottom row), 103 (top),
    105 (top, bottom), 107 (top, bottom), 108 (bottom),
    109, 111 (top-left, middle row, bottom row),
    113 (top-right, middle-left, middle-right,
    bottom-center, bottom-right), 157 (bottom-right),
    171 (top-left), 201 (bottom-right), 255 (top-center,
    bottom-right), 271 (bottom-center),
    323 (bottom-left, bottom-right), 335 (top),
    382 (bottom)

The sun sets over Neil Subin's ranch garden, which overlooks the Big Bend landscape south of Marfa.

A bouquet of gomphrena epitomizes
country charm in Jared Barnes's
Nacogdoches garden.

ACKNOWLEDGMENTS

TO THE HOMEOWNERS and designers featured here, who invited me into their gardens and shared their life stories with me, my sincere gratitude. This book would not exist without them. I am moved and inspired by their journeys as garden nurturers and by the beautiful, abundant, and meaningful gardens each one has made.

I dreamed about writing this book for years. But to bring it from "what if" to "let's *do* this" I'm indebted to many people. I thank the following for providing encouragement, advice, or inspiration: Nick McCullough, Allison McCullough, and Teresa Woodard for their remarkable book *American Roots*, which propelled me to seek out and share the stories of tenacious, forward-looking Texas gardeners; gardener-philosopher Jennifer Jewell for thinking deeply about gardens with me, offering her fresh perspective on what makes Texas gardens stand out, and introducing me to her editor at Timber Press, as well as for the inspiring example of her book *Under Western Skies*; Loree Bohl, OG blogger at *Danger Garden* and a true artist with plants, for cheering me on and sharing her experience; author and legend in her field Helen Thompson for sharing tips on location scouting and getting the photographs that tell my book's story; acclaimed photographer Rob Cardillo for his valuable advice about shooting gardens, not to mention the example of his work to aspire to; wordsmith and author Teresa Woodard again, specifically for guidance on good editorial practices as an essayist; and everyone at the Lady Bird Johnson Wildflower Center, a garden that for nearly three decades has inspired me to love Texas plants and landscapes.

For generously making time to meet with me and show me gardens—opening garden gates both metaphorically and literally—thank you to the following designers and landscape architects: Christy Ten Eyck, Patrick Boyd-Lloyd, Dave Rolston, Michael Eason, Jim Martinez and Jim Fissel, Alia Gunnell, John Hart Asher, Lorie Kinler, John Troy, David Morello, Robert Bellamy, and Laurin Lindsey and Shawn Michael.

Finding and scouting gardens that fit the criteria I was looking for, across a state as big as Texas, would not have been possible without the assistance of numerous people, many of whom I'd never met except through an email introduction, and yet who spent time and brainstorming effort making suggestions and introductions of their own. For connections, leads, information, and/or generous invitations to visit a garden, my thanks to Maggi Arendsee, Norm Arnold, Jared Barnes, Katy Barone, Jeannie Biernat, Steven Chamblee, Suzzanne Chapman, Beth Clark, Lauren Clark, Dave Creech, Lori Daul, Cynthia Deegan, Beth Dinger, Janell and Andy Eilers, John Ferguson, Christine Fitzgerald, Shirley Fox, Douglas Friedman, Greg Grant, Jan Rynda Greer, Keith Hansen, Evelyn Harding, Colleen C. Hook, John Ignacio, Justin Lacey, Alex Lahti, Linda Lehmusvirta, Christa McCall, Melody McMahon, Dany Millikin, Crystal Murray, Gudrun Opperman, Betty Perez, Jay Przyborski, Cynthia Siegel and Cliff Burke, Brenda Smith, Nancy and Bob Svoboda, Susan and Mike Wallens, and Adam Woodruff. Thanks also to Kim Tarr and Claire Anderson for the comforts of home and their guest room during a week of garden shoots in their area.

Enormous thanks to photographer Kenny Braun for leaping into this ambitious project with me, for being game to travel any distance across Texas, for a willingness to go the extra mile to get the perfect shot, and for showing me how to keep cowboy-cool in 100°F heat with a pond-dipped bandana around the neck. Memories of stalking little brown birds and getting yelled at by the get-off-my-lawn lady still make me laugh. His images convey the spirit of the gardens and make this book shine. I'm proud of the work we accomplished together.

To Jared Barnes for the use of his own beautiful photographs from his garden, I am indebted. Circumstances required me to schedule his garden shoot early in spring, just weeks after a surprise late freeze, and his photos allowed me to provide a fuller picture of the plants he's growing.

Grateful thanks to my entire team at Timber and publisher Kathryn Juergens for their embrace of my book idea, for their helpful guidance when needed, and for otherwise giving me a free hand to bring my vision for the book to life. Their editorial polishing and art design expertise turned it into the beautiful book you're now reading, and I couldn't be more thrilled. I'd like to offer special thanks to the following people: acquiring editor Stacee Lawrence for saying yes and signing me with Timber; editor Makenna Goodman for her valuable feedback on the manuscript and enthusiasm for my subject; editor Naomi Ruiz for shepherding the book through production while cheerfully answering my many questions; photo editor Sara Milhollin for her guidance on the photo shoots and selecting images for these pages; copyeditor Andrew Keys for his discerning eye and drive to make the text as clear and consistent as possible; production editor Matt Burnett for efficiently managing my book from draft into published form; designers Sarah Crumb and Sara Isasi for their creativity and attention to detail in making this book gorgeous and readable; photo editor Kevin McConnell for his meticulous work in getting hundreds of photographs ready for printing; Caroline McCulloch for her marketing expertise; and editorial assistant Nick Dysinger for his helpful communications.

A Texas-sized thank you to Lori Daul, Cat Jones, Diana Kirby, and Laura Wills—my best gardening friends who text with me daily about gardening, commiserate about crazymaking Texas weather, and share the ephemeral joys of our gardens. Their support and enthusiasm for this project kept me motivated during a scheduled-to-the-hilt nine months of travel, 27 days of photo shoots in all weather, and the inevitable snags along the way. Each of them also generously took the time to read my first draft and offer thoughtful feedback, which I took to heart. These experienced garden makers deeply understand what it is to be a Texas gardener. They have my gratitude and friendship.

I can't wrap up without thanking Jenny and David Stocker for their Rock Rose garden, one of the finest Texas gardens I've had the pleasure of spending time in, and one of my earliest garden crushes. It's the one that got away. It lives on in my memory, however, as an exceptional source of inspiration.

Finally, thanks to readers of *Digging* for their keen interest in the gardens of this beautiful state—and world. Most of all, thank you to my family for their unflagging love and support. None of this would have been possible without them.

INDEX

trellises, 64, 86, 242, 254, 284, 378

Troy, John S., 202–206, 207

try-and-try-again garden, 48–59

tulip prickly pear (*Opuntia camanchica*), 185

turfgrass, 170, 290, 326, 362

Turk (dog), 121

Turk's cap (*Malvaviscus arboreus* var. *drummondii*), 8, 64, 88, 97, 102, 106, 202, 206, 213, 215, 228, 238, 286, 297, 298, 306, 307, 316, 326, 342

   'Pam Puryear', 107

Turk's cap 'Big Momma' (*Malvaviscus drummondii* 'Big Momma'), 290, 297

turnips, 162

turtles, 232

twistleaf yucca, 88

U

umbrella sedge (*Cyperus alternifolius*), 337

Umlauf, Charles, 213

understory plants, 228–241

urbanite, 322

USDA, 216, 220

U.S. Fish and Wildlife Service, 372

U.S. House of Representatives Committee on Agriculture, 220

V

variegated American agave, 192

variegated Spanish dagger, 292

vegetable garden, 8, 148, 162, 163, 206, 208, 211, 216–227, 298–302, 338–349, 366, 368, 370

viburnum, 286, 316

vines, 64

Virginia creeper, 346, 379

vitex, 199

W

walking garden, 272–285

Waller Creek, 88

Ware, Denny, 242, 251

Ware, Suzanne, 242–246, 247

wasps, 120, 144, 168, 350, 372

water, 142, 162, 232, 372. *See also* rainwater

water bowl, 141

water-conserving landscaping, 228, 240

water feature, 78, 228–232, 298, 326, 330, 386

water lily, 356

water plants, 276

water runoff, 17, 96, 102, 228, 234, 240, 272, 280, 304, 325, 342, 354

waterwise plants, 120, 187, 228, 240, 297

Weber agave, 192

weed-barrier fabric, 96

weeds, 226, 310

Weekley, Harry, 144

well-adapted plants, 10, 17, 31, 98, 115, 187, 240, 257, 316, 325, 366

West Texas

   challenges, 115

   climate, 115

   desert garden, 172–185

   grassland garden, 130–143

   MoFN Ranch, 116–129

   native plants, 144–171

   sustainability practices, 115

West Texas Roots, 116, 176

wet-weather creek, 228, 232, 234, 298, 302, 304

whale's tongue agave (*Agave ovatifolia*), 8, 31, 110, 112, 116, 129, 144, 156, 172, 176, 177, 188, 228, 234, 240, 241, 312, 316

wheat celosia (*Celosia spicata*), 59

Wheeler's sotol, 44, 69, 87, 102, 176, 178, 188

white mistflower (*Ageratina havanensis*), 88, 97, 102, 108, 228

wild bergamot (*Monarda fistulosa*), 73

wildfire, 115

wildflowers, 10, 15, 18, 28, 31, 72, 102, 120, 162, 167, 172, 176, 177, 183, 184, 202

wildlife, 64, 72, 290, 350

wildlife habitat, 64, 142, 144, 148, 232, 258–262, 262, 266, 338, 366, 370

willowleaf aster (*Symphyotrichum praealtum*), 373, 391

windmill, 172, 180, 183

winecup (*Callirhoe digitata*), 31, 64, 69, 70

Winkler's blanketflower 'Grape Sensation' (*Gaillardia aestivalis* var. *winkleri* 'Grape Sensation'), 373

Winter Storm Uri, 13, 36, 78, 102, 242, 316, 366

Wiseman, David, 233

wisteria, 246, 251, 254

woodland garden, 206, 320

wood mulch, 32, 58, 310

woolly stemodia, 102, 107, 110, 112, 156

X

xeriscaping, 228, 240

Y

yaupon holly (*Ilex vomitoria*), 97

yellow bells (*Tecoma stans*), 120, 129, 154, 157, 183, 185

yellow cestrum (*Cestrum aurantiacum*), 297

yellow wild indigo (*Baptisia sphaerocarpa*), 368, 373

yucca, 8, 18, 36, 44, 88, 93, 94, 98, 102, 112, 120, 167, 172, 176, 202, 286, 290

   'Bright Edge', 110

Z

zinnia (*Zinnia elegans*), 158, 171, 346, 348

zoysia, 92

zucchini, 227

Apache plume's feathery
seedheads catch light like
spun sugar.

PHOTO: KENNY BRAUN

PHOTO: DIXIE FRIEND GAY

PAM PENICK has been thinking and writing about Texas gardens—as well as gardens, parks, and natural places around the world—for nearly two decades at her award-winning website, *Digging*. As a garden designer during a multi-year drought, she helped Texas homeowners transform their yards into waterwise, wildlife-friendly gardens. She's the author of *Lawn Gone! Low-Maintenance, Sustainable, Attractive Alternatives for Your Yard* (2013) and *The Water-Saving Garden: How to Grow a Gorgeous Garden with a Lot Less Water* (2016), and her work has appeared in numerous publications including *Better Homes & Gardens, Fine Gardening*, and *The American Gardener*. As the founder and host of Garden Spark, a speaker series about garden design and ecology, she fosters conversations and learning in the Austin gardening community. For more information, visit penick.net.

KENNY BRAUN is a photographer specializing in environmental portraiture and landscape and fine-art photography. He explores a sense of place and memory in his work by returning to scenes from his early years growing up in Houston, particularly the surf culture of the Texas Gulf Coast. His book *As Far as You Can See*, featuring the splendor and diversity of the Texas landscape, was published in 2018. *Surf Texas*, his book on Texas surfers and the Gulf Coast, was published in 2014. His work is included in numerous private and public collections, including the Wittliff Collections at Texas State University, and his photography has appeared in *Texas Highways, Texas Monthly, Garden & Gun, Southern Living, This Old House*, and *Wired*. He is represented by the Stephen L. Clark Gallery in Austin and the Catherine Couturier Gallery in Houston. Visit kennybraun.com for more information.